LION BRAND YARN

JUST**SCARVES**

FAVORITE PATTERNS TO KNIT AND CROCHET

EDITED BY NANCY J. THOMAS AND ADINA KLEIN

POTTER
CRAFT

NEW YORK

The author and publisher would like to thank the
Craft Yarn Council of America for providing the
yarn weight standards and accompanying icons
used in this book. For more information, please
visit www.YarnStandards.com.

Published in the United States by Potter Craft, an
imprint of the Crown Publishing Group, a division
of Random House, Inc., New York.

POTTER CRAFT and CLARKSON N. POTTER are
trademarks and POTTER and colophon are
registered trademarks of Random House, Inc.

Every effort has been made to have instructions
accurate and complete. We cannot be responsible
for variance of individual knitters (crocheters,
crafters), human errors, or typographical mistakes.

Printed in Singapore

Design by Caitlin Daniels Israel
Editors: Nancy J. Thomas and Adina Klein
Associate Design Editor: Stephanie Klose
Photography: Jack Deutsch

Library of Congress Cataloging-in-Publication Data
Lion Brand : just scarves / edited by Nancy
Thomas.
    1. Knitting—Patterns.   2. Crocheting—
Patterns.   3. Scarves.   I. Thomas, Nancy J.
TT825.L585   2005
746.43'20432—dc22   2004018931

ISBN: 1-4000-8060-6

10   9   8   7   6   5   4   3   2   1

First Edition

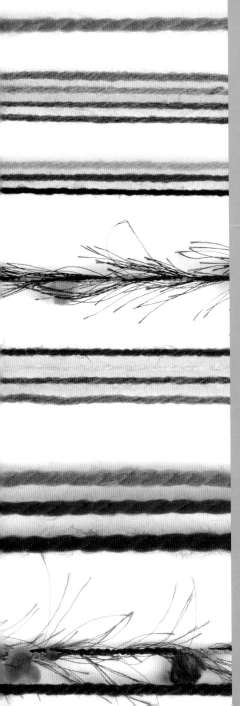

CONTENTS

INTRODUCTION 7

1. **EASY DOES IT** 18

2. **SIMPLE SCARVES WITH A TWIST** 28

3. **CABLES** 40

4. **GRANNY SQUARES** 51

5. **SHAPED SCARVES** 62

6. **LACE BASICS** 74

7. **REVERSIBLE SCARVES** 86

8. **FABULOUS SCARVES** 94

GLOSSARY 108

YARN INDEX 110

INDEX 112

INTRODUCTION

Making a scarf can be as simple as knowing
how to make a knit stitch or a single crochet.
Scarves are rewarding beginner projects
because they don't require a large time com-
mitment or great expense, making them great
"practice pieces" to try out new stitches, yarns,
and color combinations. The portability of a
small project like a scarf makes them the perfect on-the-go project. Fashionable scarves are
fun to make for yourself, but you will want to
make them for friends and family because they
make great gifts!

Just Scarves offers a variety of styles for men
and women; it teaches you a few specialized
knitting and crocheting techniques such as

making cables, lace, and perfecting granny squares, with easy-to-follow instructions and illustrations. Each chapter features fashionable and functional projects that reinforce your newly learned skills. The yarns used in this book range from fine to super bulky; and the styles range from delicate and classic to edgy and fashion-forward. Fun ways of combining yarns to create new and exciting colors and textures also are explored. The most important thing is that you are in control of your knitting and crocheting and that these projects are as fun to make as they are to wear.

There are eight chapters in this book, each with a specific focus. New knitters and crocheters will want to start with the simpler patterns in the beginning and then move their way toward the more advanced patterns in the later chapters, which feature techniques like cables (chapter three), lace (chapter six), and shaping (chapter five). However, there are easy patterns included in every single chapter, so if you know the basics, feel free to jump from chapter to chapter.

We assume that if you knit you know how to knit and purl, and if you crochet that you can single crochet, double crochet, and half double crochet. If you need to learn or refresh your memory about these basic stitches, there are a number of free resources found online and off. Learntoknit.com and learntocrochet.com offer good introductions to first-time stitchers. Crochet.about.com and knitting.about.com provide tutorials on more advanced techniques as well as forums for asking questions of the experts on staff. Most libraries have good knitting and crochet reference books and many areas have active knitting or crochet guilds that welcome new members.

We have followed the standards and guidelines created by the Craft Yarn Council of America to help you choose patterns that are right for your skill level. Each pattern is labeled as **beginner, easy, intermediate,** or **experienced. Beginner** patterns are suitable for first-time knitters and crocheters and require only basic stitch skills. **Easy** patterns call for basic stitches, repetitive pattern work, simple color changes, simple shaping, and finishing. **Intermediate** patterns include a variety of stitches (such as lacework, simple intarsia, and finishing). Projects using **advanced** techniques such as multicolor changes, complicated cables, lace patterns, fine threads, small needles and hooks, detailed shaping, and finishing are for experienced knitters and crocheters. The skill rating for each pattern is listed underneath the pattern title.

KNOWING YOUR YARNS

Scarves can be made with any yarn. Thicker yarns produce warm scarves to pair with coats and jackets. Lightweight yarns and novelty blends make nice scarves that can be worn indoors, almost like jewelry. In today's marketplace there is a dazzling variety of yarns. Knowing the inherent qualities of each type of yarn will lead you to pleasing results when you experiment with different texture combinations.

Traditional **smooth** yarns give good stitch definition and are great for trying different stitches or experimenting with color. They come in a range of gauges from super fine to extra bulky. These yarns also come in a variety of fibers and blends to fit any project or budget. Wool and wool blends are great for winter scarves. Acrylic yarns are great for people who are allergic to animal fibers or who need their garments to be machine washable. Cotton and cotton blends make great year-round scarves. Microfibers provide excellent drape and are great for shawls.

Brushed yarns give off a "halo" of hair and work well on large needles and hooks in simple stitches. They include mohair, mohair blends, angora, and synthetic yarns.

Chenille yarn looks and feels like velvet. It is best to knit and crochet these yarns at a firm gauge.

Other yarns are **heavily textured**. Bouclés, for instance, are "loopy" yarns, which can hide a multitude of stitching sins. They are best used on larger needles and hooks. Since they work up fast, they are as fun to wear as they are to make. One caution: make sure you pick up the entire thread and do not catch your needle or hook on the "loop" part of the yarn only.

Wearing a scarf made out of **eyelash yarn** is a fun way to express your inner diva. Since the "lash" part of the yarn is connected by a thinner thread, eyelash yarns can easily be worked with other yarns to produce great effects. Try combining two different colors of eyelash to create a mélange of colors.

Ribbon and **tape** are flat yarns that create interesting textures when knit or crocheted. Work them at a loose gauge for best results.

A good rule of thumb with any fancy or textured yarn is "less is more." Save the fancy stitchwork for smoother yarns. With all that dazzle already there, let the yarn do the work for you.

YARN WEIGHTS

Different people mean different things when describing yarn as "bulky" or "sportweight." The Craft Yarn Council of America has established guidelines called the Standard Yarn Weight System to standardize descriptions of yarn thickness. The materials section of each pattern in this book features an icon of a skein of yarn with a number on it. That number corresponds to one of these standards. The guiding principle of this system is: the smaller the number, the smaller the yarn.

FINDING YOUR GAUGE

Figuring out your gauge may be a new concept if you haven't been knitting or crocheting very long. In general, gauge (sometimes called tension) is the number of stitches and rows measured over a number of inches (or centimeters) of your fabric. Every knitter or crocheter has her or his own particular tension even when using the same needles and yarn as someone

STANDARD YARN WEIGHT SYSTEM

YARN WEIGHT SYMBOL & CATEGORY NAMES	1 SUPER FINE	2 FINE	3 LIGHT	4 MEDIUM	5 BULKY	6 SUPER BULKY
TYPE OF YARNS IN CATEGORY	Sock, Fingering, Baby	Sport, Baby	DK, Light Worsted	Worsted, Afghan, Aran	Chunky, Craft, Rug	Bulky, Roving
KNIT GAUGE RANGE* IN STOCKINETTE STITCH TO 4 INCHES	27–32 sts	23–26 sts	21–24 sts	16–20 sts	12–15 sts	6–11 sts
RECOMMENDED NEEDLE IN METRIC SIZE RANGE	2.25–3.25 mm	3.25–3.75 mm	3.75–4.5 mm	4.5–5.5 mm	5.5–8 mm	8 mm and larger
RECOMMENDED NEEDLE U.S. SIZE RANGE	1 to 3	3 to 5	5 to 7	7 to 9	9 to 11	11 and larger
CROCHET GAUGE* RANGES IN SINGLE CROCHET TO 4 INCH	21–32 sts	16–20 sts	12–17 sts	11–14 sts	8–11 sts	5–9 sts
RECOMMENDED HOOK IN METRIC SIZE RANGE	2.25–3.5 mm	3.5–4.5 mm	4.5–5.5 mm	5.5–6.5 mm	6.5–9 mm	9 mm and larger
RECOMMENDED HOOK U.S. SIZE RANGE	B–1 to E–4	E–4 to 7	7 to I–9	I–9 to K–10½	K–10½ to M–13	M–13 and larger

*Guidelines Only: The above reflect the most commonly used gauges and needle or hook sizes for specific yarn categories.

else, so it is important to check your gauge before beginning any project.

You will need to knit or crochet a swatch to find your gauge number. As a starting point, use the needle or crochet hook size recommended on the back of the manufacturer's yarn label. Knit or crochet a swatch in the stitch called for by your project AT LEAST 4" (10 cm) wide. It is important to make a fabric for your scarf that drapes and is not too tight and stiff. Imagine your swatch as a full-size scarf—would it be comfortable to wear? If you are not happy with the fabric, try different needle or hook sizes until you are satisfied with the results.

With a ruler, count the number of stitches in a 4" (10 cm) width (including half-stitches if there are any). Divide this number by 4, and you have your gauge number, or THE NUMBER OF STITCHES PER INCH. It is a good idea to take this measurement at a few different places on the fabric and average them. Your number may have half or quarter stitches represented (as a decimal point if you did your division on a calculator). If you did not get very close to the gauge in the pattern, go up a needle size if your gauge is too small, or down a needle size if it is too large, and try again. Now you have your gauge.

NEEDLES/HOOKS

As you become more experienced as a knitter or crocheter, you often develop a preference for a certain type of needle and hook. Needles and hooks range from plastic and metal to bamboo and exotic woods like ebony, and some are gold plated! Use what makes you most comfortable. It is sometimes beneficial to

knit back and forth on circular needles (instead of straights) because the cord connecting them can accommodate more stitches.

OTHER TOOLS

It is handy to have scissors, a tape measure, and a large-eyed, blunt needle for weaving in ends. You might find it useful to have stitch markers and cable needles for certain projects.

SIZING

Even though scarves can be and are made in any size or length, here are some general guidelines. Keep in mind that scarves tend to stretch lengthwise with wear. It's better to err on the short side and make your scarf slightly wider since it will shrink in width as it stretches. The weight of the yarn you choose will also affect the size of the scarf. A thinner scarf will wrap around a neck several times with greater ease than a bulkier one. The suggested lengths listed below do not include fringe.

GENERAL LENGTH GUIDELINES

Ages 2, 4, 6	4" x 24", 28", 32" (10 x 61, 71, 81 cm)
Ages 8–10	5" x 36" (13 x 91 cm)
Woman regular	7" x 60" (18 x 153 cm)
Woman long	4" x 72" (10 x 183 cm)
Man regular	6" x 48" (15 x 122 cm)
Man long	7" x 60" (18 x 153 cm)

SCARVES FOR KIDS

There are several important things to keep in mind when making scarves for children. First, choose your yarn wisely. Who hasn't heard a child complain about a sweater being "too itchy"? Make sure the yarn is soft enough for sensitive, growing skin. Look for yarns that are machine washable. Wool blends, acrylics, and some novelty yarns are great choices.

Be wary of long scarves, which tangle easily and can trip the wearer. A child's scarf should not hang below the waist when it is wrapped around the neck once.

Let's face it: even the most responsible child will eventually lose her scarf unless it is sewn into her coat. A child's scarf is not the item to experiment with complicated stitches on tiny needles with the finest cashmere. You might consider making a slit in the scarf (see Mighty Mini, page 29) so that it is secured around the child's neck.

Children can be just as particular as adults about what they wear. If possible, take the child with you when picking out the yarn. A scarf has a greater chance of being worn if the child has participated in its making.

Remember: scarves don't have to fit perfectly, so the most important thing is to fall in love with some yarn, grab your hooks and needles, and have fun!

FINISHING

Since both sides of a scarf are often seen, it is important to weave in ends as neatly as possible. Once you have finished your project, you may want to save a label from the yarn. That way, when it's time to wash your scarf, you can follow the manufacturer's recommendations.

FUN FINISHES

Even the simplest scarf becomes a masterpiece when you embellish it. These techniques are the tools you need to express your creativity and the personality of the wearer.

FRINGE

Probably the most common embellishment for scarves, fringe can be any length.

Certain yarns, like bouclés or anything softly spun, tend to fray when used as fringe. Don't despair; knit or crochet your fringe instead. To create a knitted fringe (like that on Muff Shawl, page 69), cast on a small number of stitches and knit in stockinette stitch for the desired length. Place these stitches on a spare piece of yarn or stitch holder and repeat until you have the number of fringes you want for the width of your scarf. Place fringe stitches on a needle and knit across row, joining the fringe as you knit. You can either continue to knit your scarf from here or bind off loosely and sew to scarf edge.

For crocheted fringe, crochet chains that are as long as you want the finished fringe. Then attach them evenly spaced along bottom edge. For looped fringe, crochet chains that are twice as long as you want the finished fringe. Fold them in half and attach evenly along bottom edge, loop side out. For looped fringe that is attached as you go, see Here's the Skinny, page 36.

To create fringe, cut lengths of yarn slightly longer than twice as long as you want the fringe. For each fringe, place three strands (more for fuller fringe, less for thinner fringe) together and fold in half. With wrong side of scarf edge facing, use a crochet hook to draw center of strands through first stitch, forming a loop (illustration 1-1). Pull ends of fringe through this loop (illustration 1-2). Pull to tighten. Continue across edge of scarf, spacing fringes evenly. Trim fringe if necessary.

The possibilities are endless. We suggest you experiment. Comb yard sales for old macramé patterns. Try using techniques from other projects on your basic scarves to give them a certain flair. The Medusa Scarf on page 30 is a perfect example: crocheted cords and bobbles become fringe.

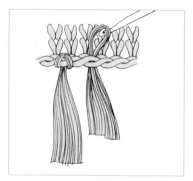

1-1. Draw strands through edge.

1-2. Pull ends of strands through the loop.

TASSELS

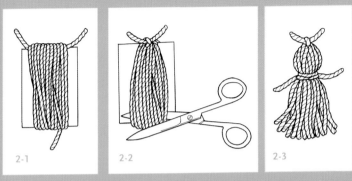

2-1

2-2

2-3

2-1 TO 2-3. Wrap yarn around cardboard, cut one end, and tie tassel.

POM-POMS

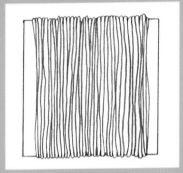

3-1. Wrap yarn around cardboard.

3-2. Cut strands at both ends.

3-3. Trim pom-pom.

TASSELS

Tassels add a dramatic finish to just about any scarf. To make a tassel, cut a piece of cardboard the length you want the finished tassel to be. Wrap yarn around cardboard, remembering that more yarn means a fuller, heavier tassel. Slip a piece of yarn under one end and tie in a knot. Cut the other end open. With a separate piece of yarn, wrap and tie tassel near top (illustrations 2-1 to 2-3).

POM-POMS

Pom-poms are not just for ski hats anymore. They can be big or little, multi-colored or solid. To make, cut a cardboard square the size you want the finished pom-pom to be. Wrap yarn loosely around cardboard (illustration 3-1). There is no hard and fast rule as to how many times to wrap, but the more wraps, the fuller the pom-pom. Also remember that the bigger the square, the more wraps you need for a full pom-pom.

Slip the yarn off the cardboard. Tie the bundle in the center and cut the loops at both ends (illustration 3-2). Fluff the yarn strands and trim if necessary (illustration 3-3).

WEAVING

A fun and easy way to spice up an otherwise plain scarf is to weave a novelty yarn through the scarf after it is finished. This is an excellent way to make economical use of novelty yarns. (See Western Weave, page 39.)

Thread a blunt, large-eyed yarn needle with desired yarn. Using a running stitch, weave decorative yarn in and out of stitches working the scarf lengthwise. Use the knitted or crocheted stitches as a guide. For example, weave over two stitches and under the next two stitches. When you have woven all the way across the piece, you can either turn and go back or cut yarn, leaving extra length for self-fringe. It is advisable to tack down yarn with sewing thread to avoid pulling.

EMBROIDERY

Chain Stitch is a simple embroidery technique that looks great on knitted and crocheted fabric because it mimics the shape of stitches. (See Vintage Vines, page 105.) Once mastered, it is easy to "draw" with this method either following a chart or working freeform. Personalize a simple scarf by embroidering the recipient's initials.

Choose a yarn smooth enough to glide through the finished fabric.

Step 1: Using a blunt, large-eyed yarn needle, secure the yarn by gently attaching it to a stitch on the wrong side of work. Leave a 3" (7.5 cm) tail for weaving in.

Step 2: Draw the needle through to the right side of the work.

Step 3: Create a small loop by inserting the needle back where it came out. Secure the loop with your finger. Pull the needle through, above the loop, creating a chain stitch (illustration 1). Do not pull too tightly or the fabric will warp. Repeat Step 3 in any direction desired, careful to space stitches evenly.

Blanket Stitch, sometimes called buttonhole stitch, is a great finishing touch on edges. (See Gentleman Caller, page 95.)

Step 1: Using a blunt, large-eyed yarn needle, secure the yarn by gently attaching it to a stitch on the wrong side of work. Leave a 3" (8 cm) tail to weave in later.

Step 2: Carefully draw the yarn needle through to the right side of work, close to the edge.

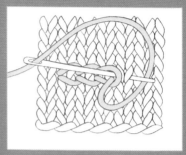

1. Chain stitch on knit fabric.

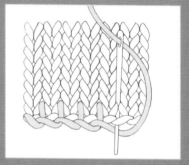

2. Blanket stitch finish.

Step 3: Bring the needle above the yarn and insert it a couple of stitches to the right of where you first inserted it (illustration 2).

Step 4: Pull the needle past the edge of the scarf to complete the stitch.

Repeat Steps 3 and 4, inserting the needle the same number of stitches apart for even spacing.

PICOT BORDER

Picots make a lovely border on lace scarves and add a feminine flair to other bulkier scarves as well. There are many variations of picot. Here are directions for a simple crochet version you can try:

In same stitch work [3 double crochet, chain 3, slip stitch in 3rd chain from hook, 3 double crochet].

Border: Work 2 double crochet in corner space. Working along edge of scarf, work as follows: single crochet in next space, (skip next space, picot in next space, skip next space, single crochet in next space).

Join round with a slip stitch in top of starting chain-3. Fasten off.

An important thing to remember when you work an edging around a corner is to work three stitches into the corner space so that the edging will round the corner smoothly and won't pull the fabric.

EMBELLISHMENTS

We have included knit and crochet instructions for basic flowers. However, the possibilities are endless.

KNIT FLOWERS

Petals (make 5): Cast on 3 stitches, knit 1 row.
Next row: Knit 1, increase 1, knit 1, increase 1 (5 stitches).
Knit 10 rows. Cut yarn and place petal on holder.
Line up petals on needle and knit across all stitches, joining them (25 stitches). Knit 1 row.
Next row: Knit 1, *knit 2 together; repeat from * across row (13 stitches).

Next row: Knit 1, *knit 2 together; repeat from * across row (7 stitches).
Cut yarn and thread through remaining stitches, drawing tight. Weave in ends.

CROCHET FLOWERS

Chain 4. Join with slip stitch to form a ring.
Round 1 Chain 1 (counts as 1 single crochet), work 11 single crochet into ring. Join round with slip stitch in chain-1.
Round 2 [Chain 3, skip next stitch, single crochet in next stitch] 6 times—6 chain-3 loops.
Round 3 [In next chain-3 loop work (single crochet, half double crochet, 3 double crochet, half double crochet, single crochet)] 6 times. Join round with a slip stitch in first single crochet. Fasten off.

1.

EASY DOES IT

So you finally learned the basics of knitting or crocheting. What can you make with your new skills? My Scarf, My Way! Knit Scarf and My Scarf, My Way! Crochet Scarf are easy-to-follow patterns that show you how to make great scarves exactly the size you want using any yarn. Just read the suggested gauge on the yarn's label, pick up the appropriate needle or hook size, and get stitching. The charts in the pattern are clear and easy to understand so you can create a customized scarf.

If you prefer to follow a pattern, we've also included two beginner-friendly projects: one knit and one crochet.

READING THE CHARTS

Once you've determined your gauge (see page 10 for instructions), decide which size scarf you want to make. When you come to a chart in your pattern, look for the size you wish to make, which is found across the row, from smallest to largest. The gauge numbers, called "G" numbers, appear down along the side, in stitches per inch. A gauge of three stitches per inch is represented by G3. Find your "G" number along the left side, then follow across to find your size. For instance, if you are making a scarf in G3 in the medium size, you would go down the column to G3, and across to M and cast on/chain 21 stitches. If there is only one column of numbers, it applies to all sizes. If there is only one row of numbers, it applies to all gauges.

MY SCARF, MY WAY!
KNIT SCARF

KNIT/BEGINNER

Skinny 4" x 96" (10 x 244 cm)
Medium 7" x 60" (18 x 153 cm)
Wide 24" x 72" (61 x 183 cm)

• Approximately 300–400 yd
(274–366 m) for Skinny and
Medium, 600–700 yd (549–640
m) for Wide. Yarn amounts will
vary due to scarf size and yarn
gauge.

• 1 pair straight needles in size
necessary to obtain gauge.

Work your gauge over garter stitch
(knit every row), following the
instructions under "Finding Your
Gauge" on page 10.

GAUGE: CAST ON (STITCHES):

	SKINNY	MEDIUM	WIDE
G1.5	6	11	36
G2	8	14	48
G2.5	10	18	60
G3	12	21	72
G3.5	14	25	84
G4	16	28	96
G4.5	18	32	108
G5	20	35	120

Work even in garter stitch until the
piece measures:

SKINNY	MEDIUM	WIDE
96"	60"	72"
244 cm	153 cm	183 cm

Bind off all stitches loosely.

Weave in ends.

MY SCARF, MY WAY! CROCHET SCARF

CROCHET/BEGINNER

SIZE

Skinny 4" x 96" (10 x 244 cm)
Medium 7" x 60" (18 x 153 cm)
Wide 24" x 72" (61 x 183 cm)

MATERIALS

- Approximately 300–450 yd (274–412 m) for Skinny and Medium, 750–850 yd (686–777 m) for Wide. Yarn amounts will vary due to scarf size and yarn gauge.

- Crochet hook in size necessary to obtain gauge.

GAUGE

Work your gauge over half double crochet, following the instructions under "Finding Your Gauge" on page 10.

SCARF

GAUGE: CHAIN:

	SKINNY	MEDIUM	WIDE
G1.25	6	10	31
G1.5	7	12	37
G2	9	15	49
G2.5	11	19	61
G3	13	22	73
G3.5	15	26	85
G4	17	29	97
G4.5	19	33	109
G5	21	36	121

Row 1 Half double crochet in the 3rd chain from the hook and each chain across—you will have one less half double crochet than the number of chains.

Row 2 Chain 2, half double crochet in each half double crochet across. Repeat Row 2 until the piece measures desired length or:

SKINNY	MEDIUM	WIDE
96"	60"	72"
244 cm	153 cm	183 cm

Fasten off.

FINISHING

Weave in ends.

AS PICTURED

WIDE: G2, WITH 4 SKEINS HOMESPUN #345 CORINTHIAN.

MEDIUM: G1.25, WITH 2 BALLS OF JIFFY THICK AND QUICK #208 ROCKY MOUNTAINS.

SKINNY: G3, WITH 3 BALLS EACH OF FUN FUR #113 RED AND #191 VIOLET, MADE WITH 2 STRANDS HELD TOGETHER THROUGHOUT.

TIE BEAUX

DESIGNED BY WENDY PRESTON

KNIT/BEGINNER

This simple ribbed scarf is brought to new heights with coordinating novelty yarn.

SIZE
5" x 48" (12.5 x 122 cm)

MATERIALS

 LION BRAND YARN WOOL-EASE CHUNKY 80% ACRYLIC, 20% WOOL 5 OZ (140 G) 153 YD (140 M) BALL

1 ball #109 Royal Blue or color of your choice

 LION BRAND YARN FANCY FUR 55% POLYAMIDE, 45% POLYESTER 1¾ OZ (50 G) 39 YD (35.5 M) BALL

1 ball #209 Brilliant Blue or color of your choice

• Size 10.5 (6.5 mm) needles *or size to obtain gauge*

• Large-eyed, blunt needle

GAUGE
14 stitches + 20 rows = 4" (10 cm) over stockinette stitch (knit on right side, purl on wrong side).
Be sure to check your gauge.

SCARF
With Fancy Fur, cast on 21 stitches and work in garter stitch (knit every row) until the piece measures 4" (10 cm), ending with a wrong side row.
Change to Wool-Ease Chunky and work ribbing patterns as follows:
Row 1 (Right Side) *Purl 3, knit 3; repeat from *, ending purl 3.
Row 2 *Knit 3, purl 3; repeat from *, ending knit 3.
Repeat Rows 1 and 2 for a rib pattern until the piece measures 44" (112 cm), or 4" (10 cm) less than the desired length.
Change to Fancy Fur and work in garter stitch for 4" (10 cm).
Bind off all stitches loosely.

FINISHING
Weave in ends.

BERRY EASY SCARF

DESIGNED BY MARIANNE FORRESTAL

CROCHET/BEGINNER

This yarn is dyed with extra long color repeats that produce long stripes when crocheted lengthwise. You get vertical stripes without changing yarns!

SIZE
6" x 60" (15 x 152 cm)

MATERIALS

 LION BRAND YARN HOMESPUN
98% ACRYLIC, 2% POLYESTER
6 OZ (170 G) 185 YD (167 M) SKEIN

2 skeins #345 Corinthian or color of your choice

• Size K-10.5 (6.5 mm) crochet hook *or size to obtain gauge*

GAUGE
12 stitches + 6 rows = 4" (10 cm).
Be sure to check your gauge.

SCARF
Chain 182.
Row 1 Double crochet in 4th chain from hook and in each chain across—180 stitches. Chain 3, turn.
Row 2 Double crochet in each stitch across. Chain 3, turn.
Repeat Row 2 for pattern stitch and work even for 7 more rows.

FINISHING
Fasten off.
Weave in ends.

2.
SIMPLE SCARVES WITH A TWIST

Using only basic stitches, the six patterns in this chapter incorporate design details and fun finishes that will add flair to your finished product. But don't be intimidated, these projects only look complex. The techniques are as simple as striping and braiding.

A word on changing colors. Whether you knit or crochet, always leave a "tail" of at least four inches (10 cm) before you cut the old yarn or add a new one.

MIGHTY MINI

DESIGNED BY MARIANNE FORRESTAL

CROCHET/BEGINNER

This is the perfect accessory for every outfit. Even if you are a beginning crocheter, you can make one of these beauties. Another plus—this scarf takes very little yarn.

SIZE
5" x 26" (12.5 x 66 cm)

MATERIALS

 LION BRAND YARN CHENILLE THICK & QUICK 91% ACRYLIC, 9% RAYON 5.6 OZ (158 G) 100 YD (91 M) SKEIN

1 skein #125 Chocolate or color of your choice

• Size P-15 (10 mm) crochet hook or size to obtain gauge

• Large-eyed, blunt needle

GAUGE
8.75 stitches + 8 rows = 4" (10 cm) over single crochet.
Be sure to check your gauge.

SCARF
Chain 12.

Row 1 Single crochet in the 2nd chain from hook and each chain across—11 stitches. Chain 1, turn.

Rows 2–44 Single crochet in each stitch across. Chain 1, turn.

Row 45 Single crochet in the first 3 stitches, chain 5, skip the next 5 stitches, single crochet in the last 3 stitches. Chain 1, turn.

Row 46 Single crochet in the first 3 stitches, work 5 single crochets in chain-5 space, single crochet in the last 3 stitches. Chain 1, turn.

Rows 47–52 Single crochet in each stitch across. Chain 1, turn. When Row 52 is completed, do not chain, fasten off.

FINISHING
Weave in ends.

MEDUSA SCARF

DESIGNED BY TRACI BUNKERS

KNIT/EASY

Funky colors jazz up easy-to-knit garter stitch stripes. When working stripe pattern, carry color up along side edge of scarf until last stripe of that color is completed, then cut color. Join new colors as needed.

SIZE

8¼" x 54½" (21 x 138 cm) (not including fringe)

MATERIALS

 LION BRAND YARN WOOL-EASE 80% ACRYLIC, 20% WOOL 3 OZ (85 G) 197 YD (187 M) BALL

1 ball each, #177 Loden (A), #171 Gold (B), #137 Fuchsia (C), #179 Chestnut Heather (D),or colors of your choice

- Size 8 (5 mm) knitting needles or size to obtain gauge
- Size H-8 (5 mm) crochet hook for fringe

GAUGE

17 stitches + 32 rows = 4" (10 cm) over garter stitch (knit every row). Be sure to check your gauge.

SCARF

With A, cast on 36 stitches. Work in garter stitch, and stripe pattern as follows: *20 rows A, 2 rows B, 4 rows A, 20 rows B, 2 rows C, 4 rows B, 20 rows C, 2 rows D, 4 rows C, 20 rows D, 2 rows A, and 4 rows D; repeat from * 3 times more, then knit 20 rows A. Bind off.

FINISHING

FUNKY FRINGE

Position the scarf so the right side is facing (the tail from the cast-on will be at the lower right corner) and the cast-on edge is at the top. **Row 1** With crochet hook, join A with a slip stitch in the first stitch of the cast-on edge, *chain 20 for fringe, work 4 half double crochet in 2nd chain from hook, slip stitch in next 18 chains, then slip stitch in the same stitch as the first slip stitch at the base of the fringe, slip stitch in next 3 stitches of the cast-on edge; repeat from * 10 times more, then slip stitch in each stitch to end. Fasten off.

Row 2 From right side, skip one garter stitch ridge from Row 1 fringe. Working in the top loop only of each garter stitch along the ridge, join B with a slip stitch in the first loop, then slip stitch in the next loop. Repeat instructions between ** of Row 1 for 11 fringes. Fasten off.

Row 3 From right side, skip one garter stitch ridge from Row 2 fringe. Working in the top loop only of each garter stitch along the ridge, join C with a slip stitch in the first loop, then slip stitch in each of the next 2 loops. Repeat instructions between ** of Row 1 for 11 fringes. Fasten off.

Row 4 From right side, skip one garter stitch ridge from Row 3 fringe. Working in the top loop only of each garter stitch along the ridge, join D with a slip stitch in the first loop. Repeat instructions between ** of Row 1 for 11 fringes. Fasten off.

Position scarf so the right side is facing and the bound-off edge is at the top. Continue to work same as for cast-on edge, working Row 1 using A, Row 2 using D, Row 3 using C and Row 4 using B. Fasten off. Weave in ends.

MEDUSA SCARF

POCKET POSSIBILITIES

DESIGNED BY WENDY PRESTON

KNIT/EASY

This scarf combines stockinette stitch with a garter stitch edging. The patch pocket is a great place for warming hands or stashing treasures.

SIZE

6" x 56" (15 x 142 cm)

MATERIALS

 LION BRAND YARN WOOL-EASE CHUNKY 80% ACRYLIC, 20% WOOL 5 OZ (140 G) 153 YD (140 M) BALL

1 ball each #127 Walnut (MC), #099 Fisherman (CC), or colors of your choice

- Size 10.5 (6.5 mm) needles *or size to obtain gauge*

- Large-eyed, blunt needle

GAUGE

14 stitches + 18 rows = 4" (10 cm) over stockinette stitch (knit on right side, purl on wrong side). *Be sure to check your gauge.*

SCARF

With MC, cast on 23 stitches. Work even in garter stitch (knit every row) for 8 rows.

PATTERN STITCH

Row 1 (Right Side) Knit.
Row 2 Knit 4, purl 15, knit 4.
Repeat these 2 rows for pattern stitch and work even until piece measures 6" (15 cm) from beginning, ending with a wrong side row. Continuing in pattern stitch, work in stripe pattern as follows: *18 rows CC and 18 rows MC; repeat from * 4 times more, then work 18 rows CC once more, ending with a wrong side row; piece should measure 50" (127 cm) from beginning. Change to MC and work in stockinette stitch for 6" (15 cm). Bind off.

POCKET

With MC, cast on 23 stitches. Work in stockinette stitch for 6" (15 cm). Bind off. Weave in ends.

FINISHING

Place pocket over last 6" (15 cm) of right side of scarf. Sew around three sides to form pocket.

THE CUDDLE

DESIGNED BY GABRIELLE PETERSON

KNIT/EASY

Knit two narrow scarves combining fur yarn and an ultrasoft microfiber yarn and partially seam them together. The resulting four-tail beauty has numerous wearing possibilities.

SIZE

8" x 40" (20.5 x 102 cm)

MATERIALS

 LION BRAND YARN FUN FUR 100% POLYESTER 1¾ OZ (50 G) 64 YD (58 M) BALL

3 balls #113 Red or color of your choice

 LION BRAND YARN MICROSPUN 100% MICROFIBER 2½ OZ (70 G) 168 YD (154 M) BALL

1 ball #113 Cherry Red or color of your choice

• Size 11 (8 mm) knitting needles or size to obtain gauge

• Stitch holder

• Large-eyed, blunt needle

GAUGE

16 stitches + 16 rows = 4" (10 cm) over stockinette stitch (knit on right side, purl on wrong side) using Fun Fur and Microspun held together.
Be sure to check your gauge.

NOTE

• Use one strand each of Fun Fur and Microspun held together throughout.

SCARF—MAKE 2

With Fun Fur and Microspun held together, cast on 32 stitches. Work even in stockinette stitch for 2" (5 cm), ending with a wrong side row.

Next Row (Right Side) Knit 14, place these stitches on holder, bind off next 4 stitches, knit 14.
Work even on 14 stitches until piece measures 20" (51 cm) from beginning, ending with a wrong side row. Bind off.

Next Row (Wrong Side) Slip 14 stitches from holder back to needle ready for a purl row. Work even on these 14 stitches until piece measures 20" (51 cm) from beginning, ending with a wrong side row. Bind off and weave in ends.

FINISHING

With right side facing, sew cast-on edges together.

HERE'S THE SKINNY

DESIGNED BY MARIANNE FORRESTAL

CROCHET/EASY

Glittery yarn in an easy crochet stitch are all you need to make this glamorous scarf. The chain fringe is an elegant detail.

SIZE

3½" x 90" (9 x 229 cm) (not including fringe)

MATERIALS

LION BRAND YARN GLITTER-SPUN 60% ACRYLIC, 13% POLYESTER, 27% CUPRO 1¾ OZ (50 G) 115 YD (105 M) BALL

2 balls #135 Bronze (A), 1 ball #170 Gold (B), 1 ball #150 Silver (C), or colors of your choice

• Size G-6 (4 mm) crochet hook *or size to obtain gauge*

GAUGE

16 stitches + 8 rows = 4" (10 cm) over Double Crochet.
Be sure to check your gauge.

SCARF

With A, chain 362.

Row 1 Double crochet in the 4th chain from the hook and each chain across—360 stitches. Fasten off, turn.

Row 2 Join B with a slip stitch in the first double crochet, chain 3, double crochet in each stitch across. Fasten off, turn.

Row 3 Join C with a slip stitch in the first double crochet, chain 3, double crochet in each stitch across. Fasten off, turn.

Row 4 Join A with a slip stitch in the first double crochet, chain 3, double crochet in each stitch across. Fasten off, turn to bottom loops of the foundation chain of Row 1.

Row 5 Join B with a slip stitch in the first bottom loop, chain 3, double crochet in each loop across. Fasten off, turn.

Row 6 Repeat Row 3.

Row 7 Repeat Row 4. At the end of row, chain 1, turn to the short edge of the scarf.

FINISHING

Work 9 single crochet evenly spaced across the short edge. Turn, chain 50, slip stitch in each of first 2 single crochet, [chain 50, slip stitch in same single crochet as the last slip stitch, slip stitch in the next single crochet] 7 times, chain 50, slip stitch in the same single crochet as the last slip stitch. Turn to the long edge of the scarf, then slip stitch in each double crochet across. Chain 1, turn to the short edge, then work 9 single crochet evenly across. Work chain loop fringe the same as for the opposite short edge. Fasten off. Join yarn with a slip stitch in the first double crochet on the unworked long edge, then slip stitch in each double crochet across. Fasten off.

WESTERN WEAVE

DESIGNED BY VLADIMIR TERIOKHAN

CROCHET/EASY

Spice up an ordinary scarf by weaving a multicolor ribbon through once it is finished. This technique is a great and economical method to highlight ribbon yarns.

SIZE

7" x 55" (18 x 140 cm)
(not including fringe)

MATERIALS

 LION BRAND YARN MICROSPUN 100% MICROFIBER ACRYLIC 2½ OZ (70 G) 168 YD (154 M) BALL

3 balls #148 Turquoise (MC) or color of your choice

 LION BRAND YARN INCREDIBLE 100% POLYAMIDE 1¾ (50 G) 110 YD (100 M) BALL

1 ball #208 Copper Penny (CC) or color of your choice

• Size G-6 (4 mm) crochet hook *or size to obtain gauge*

• Sewing needle and thread to match CC

GAUGE

24 stitches + 12 rows = 4" (10 cm) over pattern stitch using MC.
Be sure to check your gauge.

SCARF

With MC, chain 45.

Foundation Row (Wrong Side)
Double crochet in the 4th chain from the hook and in each chain across—43 stitches. Chain 3, turn.

Row 1 (Right Side) Double crochet in the first 3 stitches, *chain 1, skip next stitch, double crochet in the next 3 stitches; repeat from * to the end. Chain 3, turn.

Row 2 Double crochet in each stitch and chain-1 space across. Chain 3, turn. Repeat Rows 1 and 2 for the pattern stitch and work even until the piece measures 55" (140 cm) from beginning, ending with Row 2. Fasten off. Weave in ends.

FINISHING

WEAVING

Cut CC into 10 strands 70" (178 cm) long. With right side facing, begin at the first chain-1 space at the lower right corner. Going through the chain-1 spaces, weave the first strand under and over the rows to the top edge. Weave the 2nd strand going over and under rows to the top edge. Continue to work in this manner across, alternating weaving strands under and over, with over and under. Even up CC strands at each end of the scarf by pulling the strands slightly. Using sewing needle and thread, tack each CC strand to the side edge of the chain-1 spaces at the bottom and top edges of the scarf to secure.

3.

CABLES

Making cables is not as complicated as it looks. The important thing to remember is that cabling is just a matter of rearranging stitches with a cable needle.

CHARTS

The cable patterns in this book are presented in both text and charts. Charts are read from right to left on odd-numbered rows and from left to right on even-numbered rows. Each square is the equivalent of one stitch. The symbols in the squares correspond to a key. Some knitters find it helpful to put a piece of paper or ruler below their current chart row to avoid confusing the rows.

HOW TO KNIT CABLES

The first step in knitting a cable is slipping the required number of stitches as *if to purl* on to the cable needle. The pattern will tell you to hold the cable needle to the front (illustration 1-1) or back (illustration 2-1) of your knitting. Holding stitches to the front slants the cable to the left (illustration 1-4) and holding stitches to the back slants the cable to the right (illustration 2-4).

The next step is to knit the stitches that remain on your needle (illustrations 1-2 and 2-2). Your pattern will tell you how many stitches to work.

The last step is to work the stitches on the cable needle (illustrations 1-3 and 2-3). Some knitters like to put them back on the left needle and knit them from there. Other knitters prefer to knit them directly from the cable needle. Try both ways and see which method is most comfortable for you. Just be sure not to twist the stitches as you knit them.

HOLDING STITCHES TO THE FRONT

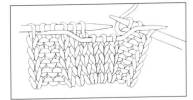

1-1. Hold stitches on a cable needle in front of work.

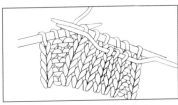

1-2. Knit remaining cable stitches.

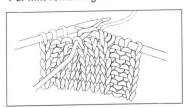

1-3. Knit stitches from cable needle.

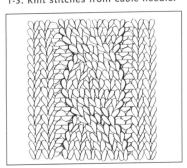

1-4. Finished front (left) cable.

HOLDING STITCHES TO THE BACK

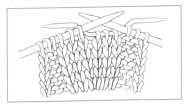

2-1. Hold stitches on a cable needle in back of work.

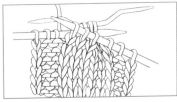

2-2. Knit remaining cable stitches.

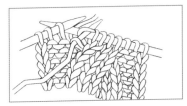

2-3. Knit stitches from cable needle.

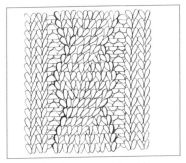

2-4. Finished back (right) cable.

BRAIDED BRANCHES

DESIGNED BY KATHY ZIMMERMAN

KNIT/EASY

This scarf is a good introduction to the world of cables. One big, bold cable knit in thick yarn means you'll be done in no time.

SIZE

5½" x 60" (14 x 153 cm)

MATERIALS

 LION BRAND YARN WOOL-EASE THICK & QUICK 80% ACRYLIC, 20% WOOL 6 OZ (170 G) 108 YD (98 M) BALL

3 balls #099 Fisherman or color of your choice

• Size 11 and 13 (8 and 9 mm) knitting needles *or size to obtain gauge*

• Cable needle

• 2 stitch markers

GAUGE

13 stitches + 16 rows = 4" (10 cm) over cable pattern using larger needles.

Be sure to check your gauge.

NOTE

• Slip markers on every row.
• For make 1 instructions, see page 64.

STITCH PATTERNS

GARTER STITCH
Knit every row.

6-STITCH RIGHT CABLE (6-ST RC)
Slip 3 stitches to cable needle and hold in back, knit 3, knit 3 from the cable needle.

6-STITCH LEFT CABLE (6-ST LC)
Slip 3 stitches to cable needle and hold in front, knit 3, knit 3 from the cable needle.

CABLE AND BORDER PATTERN
(worked over 18 stitches)
Rows 1 and 5 (Right Side) Knit.
Row 2 and All Wrong Side Rows Knit 3 (garter stitch border), purl 12, knit 3 (garter stitch border).
Row 3 Knit 6, 6-st RC, knit 6.

Row 7 Knit 3, 6-st RC, 6-st LC, knit 3.
Row 8 Repeat Row 2.
Repeat Rows 1–8 for cable and border pattern.

SCARF

With smaller needles, cast on 12 stitches. Work 4 rows in garter stitch.

Increase Row (Right Side): Knit 3 (garter st border), place marker, knit 3, [knit 1, make 1] 6 times, place marker, knit 3 (garter stitch border)—18 stitches. Change to larger needles.

Beginning with Row 2, work in cable and border pattern until piece measures 58½" (149 cm) from beginning, ending on Row 6.

Decrease Row (Right Side): Knit 3, decrease 3 stitches by placing the next 3 stitches on the cable needle and holding them in back, [knit together next stitch from left needle

CABLE AND BORDER PATTERN

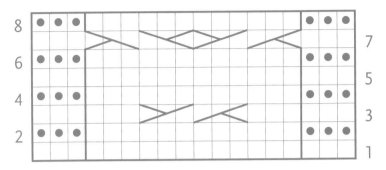

with the first stitch on the cable needle] 3 times, decrease 3 stitches by placing the next 3 stitches on the cable needle and holding them in front, [knit together next stitch from the left needle with first stitch on the cable needle] 3 times, knit 3–12 stitches. Change to smaller needles. Work 4 rows in garter stitch.

Bind off all stitches in knit 2 together method as follows: *knit 2 together, then place the resulting stitch back on the left needle; repeat from * until all stitches are bound off.

FINISHING
Weave in ends.

STITCH KEY

Knit on right side, purl on wrong side

Purl on right side, knit on wrong side

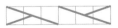

6-ST RC
Slip 3 stitches to cable needle and hold in back, knit 3, knit 3 from cable needle

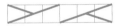

6-ST LC
Slip 3 stitches to cable needle and hold in front, knit 3, knit 3 from cable needle

CLASSIC CABLES

DESIGNED BY KATHY ZIMMERMAN

KNIT/INTERMEDIATE

Practice your stitchery with this multicabled scarf. A seed stitch border adds extra texture.

SIZE
6" x 60" (15 x 153 cm)

MATERIALS

 LION BRAND YARN FISHERMEN'S WOOL 100% PURE VIRGIN WOOL 8 OZ (224 G) 465 YD (425 M) SKEIN

1 skein #098 Natural or color of your choice.

- Size 5 and 9 (3.75 and 5.5 mm) knitting needles *or size to obtain gauge*

- Cable needle

- Stitch markers

GAUGE
32 stitches + 25 rows = 4" over cable pattern using larger needles. *Be sure to check your gauge.*

NOTE
- Slip markers on every row.

STITCH PATTERNS

4-STITCH RIGHT CABLE (4-ST RC)
Slip 2 stitches to cable needle and hold in back, knit 2, knit 2 from the cable needle.

8-STITCH RIGHT CABLE (8-ST RC)
Slip 4 stitches to cable needle and hold in front, knit 4, knit 4 from the cable needle.

SEED STITCH (OVER EVEN NUMBER OF STITCHES)
Row 1 (Wrong Side) *Knit 1, purl 1; repeat from * across.
Row 2 Purl the knit stitches and knit the purl stitches.
Repeat Row 2 for seed stitch.

TWO-CABLE PATTERN (WORKED OVER 40 STITCHES)
Row 1 (Right Side) Purl 2, 4-st RC, purl 2, [8-st RC, purl 2, 4-st RC, purl 2] twice.
Row 2 and All Wrong Side Rows Knit 2, purl 4, knit 2, [purl 8, knit 2, purl 4, knit 2] twice.

Rows 3 and 7 Purl 2, knit 4, purl 2, [knit 8, purl 2, knit 4, purl 2] twice.

Row 5 Purl 2, 4-st RC, purl 2, [knit 8, purl 2, 4-st RC, purl 2] twice.

Row 8 Repeat Row 2.

Repeat Rows 1–8 for Cable Pattern.

SCARF

With smaller needles, cast on 32 stitches.

BOTTOM BORDER

Work even in seed stitch for 7 rows.

Rows 1–5 Work in seed stitch across the first 3 stitches, knit 26, work in seed stitch across the last 3 stitches.

Row 6 Work in seed stitch across the first 3 stitches, purl 26, work in seed stitch across the last 3 stitches.

Rows 7–11 Repeat Rows 1–5.

Row 12 Repeat Row 6.

Rows 13–17 Repeat Rows 1–5.

BEGIN CABLE PATTERN

Increase Row (Wrong Side) Work in seed stitch across the first 3 stitches, place marker, purl 2, increase 1 stitch in each of the next 2 stitches as if to purl, *purl 2, increase 1 stitch in each of the next 4 stitches as if to purl, purl 2, increase 1 stitch in each of the next 2 stitches as if to purl; repeat from * once more, place marker, work in seed stitch across last 3 stitches—46 stitches. Change to larger needles.

Row 1 (Right Side) Work in seed stitch across the first 3 stitches, work Row 1 of cable pattern across next 40 stitches, work in seed stitch across the last 3 stitches. Continue to work as established until piece measures 57" (145 cm) from beginning, ending with Row 8.

Decrease Row (Right Side) Work in seed stitch across the first 3 stitches, purl 2, decrease 2 stitches by placing the next 2 stitches on the cable needle and holding them in back, [knit together next stitch from the left needle with the first stitch on the cable needle] twice, *purl 2, decrease 3 stitches by placing the next 3 stitches on the cable needle and holding in back, [knit together the next stitch from the left needle with the first stitch on the cable needle] 3 times, purl 2, decrease 2 stitches by placing the next 2 stitches on cable needle and holding in back, [knit together the next stitch from the left needle with the first stitch on the cable needle] twice; repeat from * once more, work in seed stitch across the last 3 stitches—32 stitches. Change to smaller needles.

TOP BORDER

Rows 1–4 Work in seed stitch across the first 3 stitches, knit 26, work in seed stitch across the last 3 stitches.

Row 5 Work in seed stitch across the first 3 stitches, purl 26, work in seed stitch across the last 3 stitches.

Rows 6–10 Repeat Row 1.

Row 11 Repeat Row 5.

Rows 12–16 Repeat Row 1.

Continue to work all stitches in seed stitch for 7 rows. Bind off all stitches loosely in seed stitch.

FINISHING

Weave in ends. Block lightly to measurements.

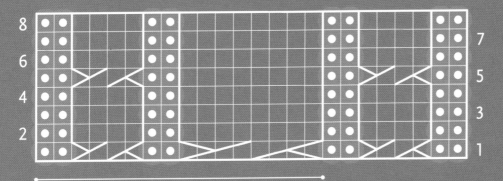

REPEAT THESE 16 STS TWICE

STITCH KEY

Knit on right side, purl on wrong side

Purl on right side, knit on wrong side

4-ST RC
Slip 2 stitches to cable needle and hold in back, knit 2, knit 2
from the cable needle

8-ST RC
Slip 4 stitches to cable needle and hold in front, knit 4, knit 4
from the cable needle

OUTRAGEOUS CABLED COLLAR

DESIGNED BY VLADIMIR TERIOKHAN

KNIT/EASY

This stylish piece can be worn over a coat on frigid days or instead of a jacket when the weather warms up. Created in a basic rectangle, this funky collar takes its shape with some cleverly placed buttons.

SIZE

38" top width x 48" bottom width x 14" long (97 x 122 x 36 cm)

MATERIALS

 LION BRAND YARN WOOL-EASE THICK & QUICK 80% ACRYLIC, 20% WOOL 6 OZ (170 G) 108 YD (98 M) BALL

4 skeins #099 Fisherman or color of your choice

- Size 11 (8 mm) 24" (61 cm) or longer circular knitting needle *or size to obtain gauge*

- Cable needle

- Stitch markers

- Three ⁷/₈" (22 mm) buttons

GAUGE

15 stitches + 11 rows = 4" (10 cm) over cable patterns.
Be sure to check your gauge.

STITCH PATTERNS

RIB PATTERN (MULTIPLE OF 2 STITCHES + 1)

Row 1 (Right Side) Knit 2, *purl 1, knit 1; repeat from *, ending purl 1, knit 2.

Row 2 Purl 2, *knit 1, purl 1; repeat from *, ending knit 1, purl 2.
Repeat Rows 1 and 2 for Rib Pattern.

6-ST CABLE (WORKED OVER 6 STITCHES)

Row 1 (Right Side) Knit 6.

Rows 2, 4 and 6 Purl 6.

Row 3 Slip 3 stitches to cable needle and hold in back, knit 3, knit 3 from the cable needle.

Rows 5 and 7 Knit 6.

Row 8 Purl 6.
Repeat Rows 1–8 for 6-stitch cable.

15-ST CABLE (WORKED OVER 15 STITCHES)

Row 1 (Right Side) Knit 15.

Rows 2, 4 and 6 Purl 15.

Row 3 Slip 5 stitches to cable needle and hold in front, knit 5, knit 5 from the cable needle, knit 5.

Row 5 Knit 15.

Row 7 Knit 5, slip 5 stitches to cable needle and hold in back, knit 5, knit 5 from the cable needle.

Row 8 Purl 15.
Repeat Rows 1–8 for 15-stitch cable.

COLLAR

Cast on 131 stitches. Work in rib pattern for 4 rows, ending with a wrong side row.

Increase Row (Right Side) Knit 2, purl 1, knit 1, place marker, [purl 2, knit 2, make 1, knit 3, purl 2, knit 7, make 1, knit 7] twice, purl 2, knit 2, make 1, knit 3, purl 2, knit 5, make 1, knit 4, make 1, knit 4, repeat between [ ] twice, purl 2, knit 2, make 1, knit 3, purl 2, place marker, knit 1, purl 1, knit 2—143 stitches.

BEGIN CABLE PATTERNS

Next Row (Wrong Side) Purl 2, knit 1, purl 1, slip marker, working Row 2 of each cable pattern, work [knit 2, 6-st cable, knit 2, 15-stitch cable] 5 times, knit 2, 6-stitch cable, knit 2, slip marker, purl 1, knit 1, purl 2. Keeping the stitches at each edge in rib pattern as established, work 2 stitches between each cable in reverse stockinette stitch (purl on right side, knit on wrong side). Work even until piece measures 13" (33 cm) from beginning, ending with a wrong side row.

Decrease Row (Right Side) Knit 2, purl 1, knit 1, slip marker, [purl 2, (knit 2 together) 3 times, purl 2, knit 5, knit 2 together, knit 1, knit 2 together, knit 5] 5 times, purl 2, [knit 2 together] 3 times, purl 2, slip marker, knit 1, purl 1, knit 2—115 stitches. Beginning with Row 2, work in rib pattern for 5 rows.
Bind off loosely in rib pattern.

FINISHING

Weave in ends. Position collar so the right side is facing and the cast-on edge is at the bottom. Sew the first button to upper left corner, 1/2" (1 cm) from the top edge and 1/2" (1 cm) from the left side edge. Sew the second button 8 1/2" (22 cm) from the top edge and 1/2" (1 cm) from the left side edge. Sew the third button 8 1/2" (22 cm) from the left side edge and 1/2" (1 cm) from the top edge.

OUTRAGEOUS CABLED COLLAR

4.
GRANNY SQUARES

Originating in the United States, granny squares were created to use up leftover yarns in the same way patchwork quilts were created to give purpose to fabric scraps. Using single or multiple colors, granny squares are satisfying and portable projects. They can be made individually and attached when all the squares are completed or attached to each other as they are made. Either way, they are far too cool to be used just for leftovers.

HOW TO CROCHET GRANNY SQUARES

Forming a ring is the first step. Chain as many stitches as the pattern dictates, insert the hook into the first chain below the slip knot (illustration 1-1), yarn over the hook and pull through the first chain and the chain on the hook (illustration 1-2).

Working into the ring (or under the chain): After you have created the ring, chain 3 chains if you are using double crochet, yarn over and insert the hook **under the ring,** yarn over and pull up a stitch. When you are working your third or larger rounds, make sure you insert your hook completely underneath the chain below it (illustration 1-3).

A handy tip when you begin each round is to hold the tail yarn on top of the chain you are crocheting into and crochet over the tail so it is tucked into the chain. This secures the tails as you work, so that you don't have to weave them later. It is a good idea to do this as you go so you won't be faced with dozens of ends to weave in when you have finished your project and are anxious to show it off.

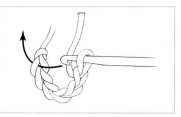

1-1. Make a chain and insert the hook into the first chain.

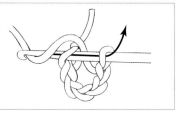

1-2. Place the yarn over the hook and pull the yarn through.

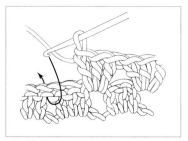

1-3. Inserting the hook underneath the previous chain or chains.

JOINING AS YOU GO ALONG

Complete one square. Begin the final round of your second square in one of the four corners. After you have completed 3 double crochets, chain 3 and take the hook out of the loop, insert it underneath the chain-3 corner of the first square, put the loop back on the hook and make 3 double crochets. Repeat this technique each time you chain 3 on the new square.

JOINING AT THE END

INVISIBLE SEAMING WITH A NEEDLE

This method produces a flat seam. Line up the piece with the right sides facing out. Attach the yarn at the lower edge without making a knot. Start on one side and insert your needle into the opposite side of the work and draw through (illustration 2-1). Alternate sides as you work up the seam (illustration 2-2).

SLIP STITCH SEAM

Work on the wrong side with the right sides of the piece facing each other. Insert the crochet hook through both fabrics, place the yarn over the hook and draw the hook through the seam and the loop on the hook (illustration 2-3).

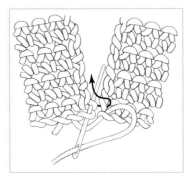

2-1. Alternate yarn on one side and insert the needle into the opposite side.

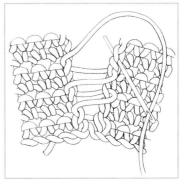

2-2. Alternate the sides up the seam.

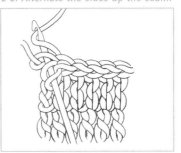

2-3. Slip stitch crochet seam.

GRANNY ON AN ANGLE

DESIGNED BY MARIANNE FORRESTAL

CROCHET/EASY

Make a contemporary granny square scarf by using two strands of one multipatterned yarn held together. Each block is made from the most basic granny pattern, then edged with one row of single crochet. Stitch them together at angles and voilà!

SIZE
8" x 50" (20.5 x 127 cm)

MATERIALS
 LION BRAND YARN MAGIC STRIPES 75% SUPERWASH WOOL, 25% NYLON 3½ OZ (100 G) 330 YD (300 M) BALL

2 balls #201 Denim Stripe or color of your choice

• Size J-10 (6 mm) crochet hook *or size to obtain gauge*

• Large-eyed, blunt needle

GAUGE
1 square = 4" (10 cm) using 2 strands held together.
Be sure to check your gauge.

NOTE
• Work two strands of yarn held together throughout.

SQUARE—MAKE 17
With 2 strands of yarn held together, chain 4, slip stitch in the 4th chain from the hook to form a ring, chain 3.

Round 1 Work 2 double crochet into the ring, chain 2, [3 double crochet into the ring, chain 2] 3 times, slip stitch in the top of the starting chain-3.

Round 2 Slip stitch in the next 2 double crochet and chain-2 space, chain 3, work 2 double crochet, chain 2, 3 double crochet in the same chain-2 space, skip the next 3 double crochet, chain 1, [(3 double crochet, chain 2, 3 double crochet) all in the next chain-2 space, chain 1, skip next 3 double crochet] 3 times, join with a slip stitch in the top of starting chain-3.

Round 3 Slip stitch in the next 2 double crochet and chain-2 space, chain 3, work 2 double crochet, chain 2, 3 double crochet in the same chain-2 space, skip the next 3 double crochet, chain 1, 3 double crochet in the next chain-1 space, chain 1, skip the next 3 double crochet, * work (3 double crochet, chain 2, 3 double crochet) all in the next chain-2 space, chain 1, skip the next 3 double crochet, work 3 double crochet in next chain-1 space, chain 1, skip the next 3 double crochet; repeat from * twice more, join with slip stitch in the top of starting chain-3. Fasten off.

SCARF
Whipstitch squares together following assembly diagram.

FINISHING
BORDER
Join yarn with slip stitch in the corner chain-2 space at either end of

scarf, work 2 single crochet in the same space, single crochet in each double crochet and chain-1 space and 2 single crochet in each corner chain-2 space to first joining. Insert hook into the corner chain-2 space on the first square, yarn over and draw through a loop, insert hook into the corner chain-2 space on the next square, yarn over and draw through a loop, yarn over and draw through all 3 loops on hook (decrease made).
Continue working around in pattern with single crochet in each double crochet and chain-1 space, work 2 single crochet in each chain-2 corner and decrease at each joining of 2 squares. Join the round with a slip stitch in the first single crochet.
Fasten off and weave in ends.

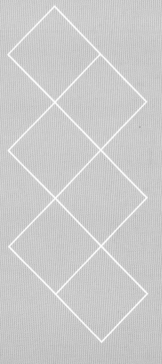

GRANNY AS YOU GO

DESIGNED BY MARIANNE FORRESTAL

CROCHET/EASY

Instead of sewing the squares together when you're done, try this method of joining them as you crochet the last round. You'll be wearing this scarf in no time.

SIZE
5" x 60" (12.5 x 153 cm)

MATERIALS

 LION BRAND YARN WOOL-EASE 80% ACRYLIC, 20% WOOL 3 OZ (85 G) 197 YD (180 M) BALL

1 ball each #098 Natural Heather (A), #130 Green Heather (B), #127 Mink Brown (C), #139 Dark Rose Heather (D), or colors of your choice

• Size G-6 (4 mm) crochet hook *or size to obtain gauge*

GAUGE
One square = 4½" (11.5 cm).
Be sure to check your gauge.

NOTE

• Squares are joined together as you work the last round.

COLOR SEQUENCE

Squares 1, 4, 7, 10, and 13 Round 1 B, Round 2 A, Rounds 3 and 4 C, Round 5 A.

Squares 2, 5, 8, and 11 Round 1 D, Round 2 A, Rounds 3 and 4 B, Round 5 A.

Squares 3, 6, 9, and 12 Round 1 C, Round 2 A, Rounds 3 and 4 D, Round 5 A.

SCARF

SQUARE 1

Note All rounds are worked from the right side.

Round 1 With A, chain 4, join chain with a slip stitch forming a ring. Chain 3 (counts as 1 double crochet), work 15 double crochet into the ring. Join round with a slip stitch in the top of the beginning chain-3. Fasten off.

Round 2 Join B with a slip stitch in any double crochet, chain 5 (counts as 1 double crochet and chain 2), [double crochet in next double crochet, chain 2] 15 times. Join the round with a slip stitch in the third chain of the beginning chain-5. Fasten off.

Round 3 Join C with a slip stitch in any chain-2 space, chain 1, single crochet in same space, chain 3, [single crochet in the next chain-2 space, chain 3] 15 times. Join the round with a slip stitch in the first single crochet. Do not fasten off.

Round 4 Slip stitch in the next chain-3 space, chain 3 (counts as 1 double crochet), work (2 double crochet, chain 3, 3 double crochet) in the same space, [3 double crochet in the next chain-3 space] 3 times, *work (3 double crochet, chain 3, 3 double crochet) in the next chain-3 space, [3 double crochet in the next chain-3 space] 3 times, repeat from * twice more. Join round with a slip stitch in the top of the beginning chain-3. Fasten off.

Round 5 Join A with a slip stitch in any chain-3 corner space, chain 1, work (single crochet, chain 3, single crochet) in the same space, chain 3, [single crochet between next two 3-double crochet groups, chain 3] 4 times, *work (single crochet, chain 3, single crochet) in the next corner chain-3 space, chain 3, [single crochet between the next two 3-double crochet groups, chain 3] 4 times; repeat from * twice more. Join the round with a slip stitch in the first single crochet. Fasten off.

SQUARE 2

Repeat Rounds 1–4 of Square 1.

JOINING

Round 5 Join A with a slip stitch in any chain-3 corner space, chain 1, single crochet in the same space, chain 1. With wrong side facing, hold Square 1 behind Square 2. Slip stitch in corresponding chain-3

corner space of Square 1, chain 1, single crochet in same chain-3 corner as last single crochet of Square 2, *chain 1, slip stitch in the next chain-3 space of Square 1, chain 1, single crochet between the next two 3-double crochet groups of Square 2; repeat from * 3 times more, chain 1, slip stitch in the next chain-3 space of Square 1, chain 1, single crochet in the next corner chain-3 space of Square 2, chain 1, slip stitch in the next corner chain-3 space of Square 1, chain 1, single crochet in the same corner chain-3 space of Square 2. Following Round 5 of Square 1, continue working around rest of Square 2, working pattern between **.

SQUARES 3–13

Work each square same as for Square 2. When working Round 5 (joining round) the last square joined is now called Square 1 and the square being joined is now called Square 2. After joining Square 13, do not fasten off.

EDGING

Chain 1, work 2 single crochet in the next chain-3 corner space of Square 13, work 2 single crochet in

the next chain-3 corner space of Square 12, work 3 single crochet in each of the next 5 chain-3 spaces, *work 2 single crochet in each of the next 2 chain-3 corner spaces, work 3 single crochet in each of the next 5 chain-3 spaces; repeat from * to last corner chain-3 space of Square 1, work 3 single crochet in this space, work 3 single crochet in each of the next 5 chain-3 spaces, work 3 single crochet in next corner chain-3 space, work 3 single crochet in each of the next 5 chain-3 spaces, **work 2 single crochet in each of the next 2 chain-3 corner spaces, work 3 single crochet in each of the next 5 chain-3 spaces; repeat from ** to last corner chain-3 space of Square 13, work 3 single crochet in this space, work 3 single crochet in each of the next 5 chain-3 spaces, work 3 single crochet in next corner chain-3 space, work 3 single crochet in each chain-3 space to beginning single crochet. Join the round with a slip stitch in the beginning single crochet.

FINISHING

Fasten off and weave in ends.

GRAPE GRANNY

DESIGNED BY LIDIA KARABINECH

CROCHET/INTERMEDIATE

Be prepared for compliments when you wear this beautiful shawl. It is made in a combination of granny squares and solid double-crochet mesh.

SIZE
64" x 34" (163 x 86 cm)

MATERIALS

 LION BRAND YARN WOOL-EASE 80% ACRYLIC, 20% WOOL 3 OZ (85 G) 197 YD (180 M) BALL

2 balls each #147 Purple (A), #153 Black (B), #143 Lavender (C), or colors of your choice

• Size J-10 (6 mm) crochet hook *or size to obtain gauge*

• Large-eyed, blunt needle

GAUGE
Large square = 5½" (14 cm). *Be sure to check your gauge.*

NOTE
• To change colors at the end of a row, draw the new color through the last 2 loops on hook to complete last double crochet, then chain 3 and turn.

SHAWL
With A, chain 4. Join chain with a slip stitch in the first chain, forming a ring.

Row 1 (Right Side) Chain 3 (always counts as 1 double crochet), work 2 double crochet, chain 3, work 3 double crochet into the ring. Chain 3, turn.

Row 2 Work 2 double crochet in the first double crochet, in the chain-3 space work (3 double crochet, chain 3, 3 double crochet), work 3 double crochet in the 3rd chain of the chain-3 of the row below. Chain 3, turn.

Row 3 Work 2 double crochet in the first double crochet, work 3 double crochet in the space between the next 3-double crochet groups, in the chain-3 space work (3 double crochet, chain 3, 3 double crochet), work 3 double crochet in the space between the next 3-double crochet groups, work 3 double crochet in the 3rd chain of chain-3 of the row below; join B. Chain 3, turn.

Row 4 Work 2 double crochet in the first double crochet, [work 3 double crochet in the space between the next 3-double crochet groups] twice, in the chain-3 space work (3 double crochet, chain 3, 3 double crochet), [work 3 double crochet in the space between the next 3-double crochet groups] twice, work 3 double crochet in the 3rd chain of the chain-3 of the row below. Chain 3, turn.

Row 5 Work 2 double crochet in the

first double crochet, [work 3 double crochet in the space between the next 3-double crochet groups] 3 times, in the chain-3 space work (3 double crochet, chain 3, 3 double crochet), [work 3 double crochet in the space between the next 3-double crochet groups] 3 times, work 3 double crochet in the 3rd chain of chain-3 of the row below; join C. Chain 3, turn.

Row 6 Work 2 double crochet in the first double crochet, work 3 double crochet in each space between the 3-double crochet groups to chain-3 space, in the chain-3 space work (3 double crochet, chain 3, 3 double crochet), work 3 double crochet in each space between the 3-double crochet groups across, end work 3 double crochet in the 3rd chain of chain-3 of the row below. Chain 3, turn.

Repeat Row 6 for pattern stitch and work in color sequence as follows: 2 rows B, 4 rows C, 4 rows A, 3 rows B, 4 rows A, 4 rows C, 2 rows B, 1 row C, and 3 rows A.

LARGE SQUARE—MAKE 1

With A, chain 4. Join chain with a slip stitch in the first chain forming a ring.

Round 1 (Right Side) Chain 3 (always counts as 1 double crochet), work 2 double crochet in the ring, chain 2, * work 3 double crochet in the ring, chain 2; repeat from * 2 more times. Join round with a slip stitch in 3rd chain of beginning chain-3. Fasten off.

Round 2 With right side facing, join B with a slip stitch in any chain-2 space. Chain 3, work 2 double crochet in the same chain-2 space, chain 1, * work (3 double crochet, chain 2, 3 double crochet) in the next chain-2 space, chain 1; repeat from * 2 more times, end with 3 double crochet in the beginning chain-2 space, chain 2. Join round with a slip stitch in the 3rd chain of beginning chain-3. Fasten off.

Round 3 With right side facing, join C with a slip stitch in any chain-2 space. Chain 3, work 2 double crochet in the same chain-2 space, chain 1, * work 3 double crochet in the next chain-1 space, chain 1, work (3 double crochet, chain 2, 3 double crochet) in the next chain-2 space, chain 1; repeat from * 2 more times, end with 3 double crochet in the next chain-1 space, chain 1, 3 double crochet in beginning chain-2 space, chain 2. Join

round with a slip stitch in the 3rd chain of the beginning chain-3. Fasten off.

Round 4 With right side facing, join B with a slip stitch in any chain-2 space. Chain 3, work 2 double crochet in the same chain-2 space, chain 1, * [work 3 double crochet in the next chain-1 space, chain 1] twice, work (3 double crochet, chain 2, 3 double crochet) in the next chain-2 space, chain 1; repeat from * 2 more times, end with [3 double crochet in the next chain-1 space, chain 1] twice, 3 double crochet in the beginning chain-2 space, chain 2. Join the round with a slip stitch in the 3rd chain of the beginning chain-3. Fasten off.

Round 5 With right side facing, join A with a slip stitch in any chain-2 space. Chain 3, work 2 double crochet in the same chain-2 space, chain 1, * [work 3 double crochet in the next chain-1 space, chain 1] 3 times, work (3 double crochet, chain 2, 3 double crochet) in the next chain-2 space, chain 1; repeat from * 2 more times, end round with [3 double crochet in next chain-1 space, chain 1] 3 times, 3 double crochet in the beginning chain-2 space, chain 2. Join round with a slip stitch in the third chain of the beginning chain-3.

Round 6 With right side facing, join B with a slip stitch in any chain-2 space. Chain 3, work 2 double crochet in the same chain-2 space, chain 1, * [work 3 double crochet in the next chain-1 space, chain 1] 4 times, work (3 double crochet, chain 2, 3 double crochet) in the next chain-2 space, chain 1; repeat from * 2 more times, end round with [3 double crochet in next chain-1 space, chain 1] 4 times, 3 double crochet in the beginning chain-2 space, chain 2. Join round with a slip stitch in the third chain of the beginning chain-3. Fasten off leaving a long tail for sewing.

SMALL SQUARE 1—MAKE 24

Work Rounds 1–3 same as for large square in the color sequence as follows: Round 1 A, Round 2 C, Round 3 B. Fasten off the last round leaving a long tail for sewing.

SMALL SQUARE 2—MAKE 22

Work Rounds 1–3 same as for large square in the color sequence as follows: Round 1 C, Round 2 A, Round 3 B. Fasten off the last round leaving a long tail for sewing.

SMALL HALF-SQUARES—MAKE 4

Work Rows 1–3 same as for Shawl in the color sequence as follows: Row 1 C, Row 2 A, Row 3 B. Fasten off the last row leaving a long tail for sewing.

FINISHING

Referring to assembly diagram, sew squares and triangles together to form border, then sew border to Shawl.

EDGING

With right side facing, join B with a slip stitch in the chain-2 space of the large square.

Round 1 Chain 1, making sure that the work lies flat, single crochet evenly around entire edge, working 3 single crochet in each corner. Join the round with a slip stitch in the first single crochet. Fasten off.

FRINGE

Cut B into 16" (40.5 cm)-lengths. For each fringe, place 3 strands together and fold in half. With the wrong side of the bottom edge facing, draw the center of the strands through chain-2 space of the large square forming a loop. Pull ends of fringe through this loop. Pull ends to tighten. Continue to attach the fringe between 3-double crochet groups across and in each chain-2 space of the small squares and in each chain-3 space of the small triangles. Trim fringe to even off, if necessary.

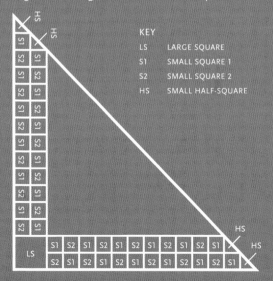

KEY
LS   LARGE SQUARE
S1   SMALL SQUARE 1
S2   SMALL SQUARE 2
HS   SMALL HALF-SQUARE

5.
SHAPED SCARVES

Simple shaping can make a plain scarf interesting and an interesting scarf extraordinary. You can create scarves and shawls in a variety of shapes, sizes, and styles once you know how to increase and decrease (detailed instructions are on pages 64 and 65). By increasing stitches at each end on alternate rows, you can easily turn a triangular scarf into a shawl. Increasing more frequently makes a long, narrow triangle, while increasing less often produces a wider triangle. Or, if you prefer, you can make bias scarves by increasing at one end of the scarf and decreasing on the other end, producing an angled piece. Some shaping at the back neck can keep a slinky scarf in place or keep a wide or bulky scarf from bunching up uncomfortably.

PLAIN AND FANCY

DESIGNED BY REBECCA ROSEN

KNIT/EASY

Customizing this scarf is a snap: just increase at the beginning of each row until it's as big as you want it.

SIZE
22" x 46" (56 x 117 cm)

MATERIALS

LION BRAND YARN FANCY FUR
55% POLYAMIDE, 45% POLYESTER
1¾ OZ (50 G) 39 YD (35.5 M)
BALL

6 balls #253 Bold Black or color of your choice

• Size 13 (9 mm) needles *or size to obtain gauge*

• Stitch markers

GAUGE
12 stitches + 16 rows = 4" (10 cm) over garter stitch (knit every row). *Be sure to check your gauge.*

SCARF

Cast on 3 stitches.

Row 1 (Right Side) Knit 1, yarn over (see page 76), place marker, knit 1, place marker, yarn over, knit 1.

Row 2 Knit 1, yarn over, knit 1, slip marker, purl 1, slip marker, knit 2.

Row 3 Knit 1, yarn over, knit to the first marker, slip marker, knit 1, slip marker, knit to end of row.

Row 4 Knit 1, yarn over, knit to the first marker, slip marker, purl 1, slip marker, knit to end of row.

Repeat Rows 3 and 4 until the center of the scarf measures 22" (56 cm) long.

Bind off all stitches loosely as if to knit.

FINISHING
Weave in ends.

INCREASING AND DECREASING IN KNITTING

The two most common ways of increasing without leaving a hole are the make one increase and knitting in the front and back of a stitch.

To work the make one increase, insert the tip of the left needle from front to back under the strand between your right and left needles (illustration 1-1). Twist this strand (illustration 1-2) and by knitting into the back of the stitch.

To knit into the front and back of a stitch, begin by knitting the stitch normally (illustration 2-1). Before you slip it off the left needle, bring the right needle around to the back of the left needle and knit into the back of the stitch (illustration 2-2). For information on decreases see chapter six, Lace Basics, on page 76.

When it comes to keeping track of increases and decreases, safety pins are a knitter or crocheter's best friend. Need to increase on the right side only? When you're making a reversible scarf or working with textured yarn, it can be difficult to tell which side is which. Attach a large safety pin on the right side of the work and you'll always know where you are. A piece of contrasting yarn will also work in a pinch.

If you need to do a certain number of decreases, don't bother with constant counting and recounting. Set aside the same number of safety pins and attach one to your scarf every time you decrease. When you run out of pins, you're done!

MAKE ONE

1-1. Make one by inserting the needle into the strand.

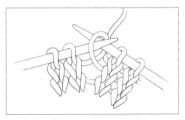

1-2. Knit into the back of the stitch.

KNIT INTO THE FRONT AND BACK OF A STITCH

2-1. Knit into the front of the stitch.

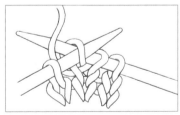

2-2. Leaving the stitch on the needle, knit into the back of the stitch.

INCREASING AND DECREASING IN CROCHET

The ever-popular ripple stitch (sometimes called chevron) uses increases and decreases in a row to produce an undulating fabric. Its zigzag nature creates a serrated edge and its reversibility makes it perfect for scarves, wraps, and afghans.

Ripple patterns are made in "multiples" that repeat across the row. Often a pattern will be a multiple of a particular number plus some extra stitches. These extra stitches provide balance in the pattern so that your piece will begin and end symmetrically. After you have created the foundation chain, it is advisable to use markers between the multiples as you set up your pattern.

Ripple patterns increase stitches by working more than one stitch in a space and decrease stitches by working two stitches together.

Increase a stitch (shown here in single crochet) by working a stitch into a space and then inserting the hook into the same space (illustration 1-1). Work a second stitch into the same space (illustrations 1-2 and 1-3). On the next row, make single crochets above both stitches.

Decrease a stitch (shown here in single crochet) by pulling up a loop in one space and then a second loop in the next space (illustration 2-1). Place the yarn over the hook and draw through all 3 loops on the hook (illustration 2-2). One stitch is decreased (illustration 2-3).

INCREASING

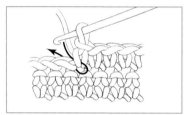

1-1. Work one stitch in a space.

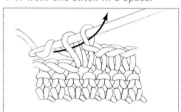

1-2. Make a second stitch in the same space.

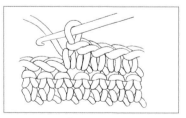

1-3. One stitch is increased.

DECREASING

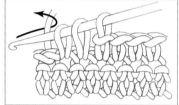

2-1. Pull up a loop in two spaces.

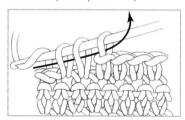

2-2. Place the yarn over the hook and draw through all 3 loops.

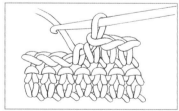

2-3. One stitch is decreased.

GARTER DIAMONDS

DESIGNED BY STEPHANIE KLOSE

KNIT/EASY

Simple increases and decreases shape this garter stitch scarf. Vary the size of your diamonds for extra panache.

SIZE
6½" x 65" (16.5 x 165 cm)

MATERIALS
 LION BRAND YARN HOMESPUN
98% ACRYLIC, 2% POLYESTER
6 OZ (170 G) 185 YD (169 M)
SKEIN

1 skein #355 Delft or color of your choice

• Size 11 (8 mm) needles *or size to obtain gauge*

GAUGE
12 stitches + 20 rows = 4" (10 cm) over garter stitch (knit every row). *Be sure to check your gauge.*

SCARF

SET UP DIAMOND PATTERN
Cast on 3 stitches.
Knit 1 row.
Next Row (Right Side) Knit into the front and back of the first stitch, knit 1, knit into the front and back of the last stitch—5 stitches.
Knit next row.

BEGIN DIAMOND PATTERN
Row 1 (Right Side) Knit 1, knit into the front and back of the next stitch, knit to last 2 stitches, knit into the front and back of the next stitch, knit 1.
Row 2 Knit.

Rows 3–14 Repeat Rows 1 and 2—19 stitches.
Row 15 Knit 1, *knit next stitch, wrapping the yarn twice around the needle; repeat from *, end row knit 1.
Row 16 Knit all stitches, dropping extra wraps.
Row 17 Knit 1, knit 2 together, knit to last 3 stitches, knit 2 together, knit 1.
Row 18 Knit.
Rows 19–30 Repeat Rows 17 and 18—5 stitches.
Repeat Rows 1–30 seven times more.
Last Row Knit 1, knit 2 together, knit 2 together—3 stitches.
Bind off.

FINISHING
Weave in ends.

MUFF SHAWL

DESIGNED BY VLADIMIR TERIOKHAN

KNIT/INTERMEDIATE

Vintage glamour! You'll feel like a 1930s movie star in this elegant wrap with handwarmer pocket and luxuriant fringe.

SIZE
13" wide x 41½" from center back neck to start of fringe (33 x 105.5 cm)

MATERIALS

 LION BRAND YARN COLOR WAVES 83% ACRYLIC, 17% POLYESTER 3 OZ (85 G) 125 YD (113 M) SKEIN

4 skeins of #353 Lava or color of your choice

- Size 9 (5.5 mm) knitting needles *or size to obtain gauge*

- Stitch holders

GAUGE
11.25 stitches + 20 rows = 4" (10 cm) over stockinette stitch (knit on right side, purl on wrong side). *Be sure to check your gauge.*

SHAWL
RIGHT FRONT FRINGE
Cast on 5 stitches.
Work even in stockinette stitch until the piece measures 5½" (14 cm), ending with a wrong side row. Break yarn and place stitches on holder.
Repeat 7 times more; do not place last fringe on holder or break yarn.

FRONT
First Shawl Row (Right Side) Knit 4, purl 1 across first fringe. *Place 1 fringe from holder on left needle, then work across as follows: purl 1, knit 3, purl 1. Repeat from * across all but the last fringe. Place the last fringe on the left needle, then work across row as follows: purl 1, knit 4—40 stitches.
Next Row (Wrong Side) Purl 4, *knit 2, purl 3; repeat from * to last 6 stitches, end row with knit 2, purl 4. Continue in rib as established for

1½" (4 cm) from the first shawl row, ending with a wrong side row.
Next Row (Right Side) Knit 1, purl 1, knit 1, purl 1, knit to last 4 stitches, purl 1, knit 1, purl 1, knit 1. Continue as established, working rib over the first and last 4 stitches and stockinette stitch over the center stitches, until the piece measures 31" (79 cm) from first shawl row, ending with a right side row.
Next Row (Wrong Side) Bind off 4 stitches at beginning of row, work to end. Work 1 row even. Continue to bind off 4 stitches at the beginning of each wrong side row until all the stitches are bound off.

MUFF
Cast on 26 stitches.
Row 1 Knit.
Row 2 Knit 3, purl 20, knit 3. Continue as established, working garter stitch (knit every row) over the first and last 3 stitches and

stockinette stitch over the center 20 stitches until the piece measures 6" (15 cm). Bind off all stitches loosely.

LEFT FRONT

Work same as for right front until piece measures 31" (79 cm) from the first shawl row, ending with a wrong side row.

Next Row (Right Side) Bind off 4 stitches at the beginning of the row, work to end.

Work 1 row even.

Continue to bind off 4 stitches at the beginning of each right side row until all the stitches are bound off.

BACK

Cast on 59 stitches.

Row 1 Knit 1, *purl 2, knit 3; repeat from * across to last 3 stitches, purl 2, knit 1.

Row 2 Purl 1, *knit 2, purl 3; repeat from * across to last 3 stitches, knit 2, purl 1.

Continue in rib as established for 1½" (4 cm), ending with a wrong side row.

Change to stockinette stitch and work even until the back piece measures 3" (8 cm), ending with a wrong side row.

Next (Decrease) Row (Right Side) Knit 2, slip, slip, knit (see Glossary, page 109), work to last 4 stitches, knit 2 together, knit 2.

Work 3 rows even.

Repeat the last 4 rows 9 times more.

Repeat decrease row once more—37 stitches.

Work even until the piece measures 12" (30 cm).

SHOULDER SHAPING

Bind off 2 stitches at the beginning of the next 10 rows.

Bind off remaining 17 stitches.

FINISHING

Sew muff to left front as follows: Center muff between the side edges and place the bottom edge 11" (28 cm) up from the first shawl row. Sew down top and bottom edges. Sew top of left front and right front to sides of back, matching the first front bind-off with the bottom of the back, and the last front bind-off with the last shoulder shaping of the back. Weave in ends.

CHEVRON IN A JIFFY

DESIGNED BY MARIANNE FORRESTAL

CROCHET/EASY

Crocheting a scarf lengthwise always seems to go faster—there are so few rows! This fashionably skinny scarf is fun to make with extra thick yarn and a giant-sized crochet hook.

SIZE
4" x 90" (10 x 229 cm)

MATERIALS

 LION BRAND YARN JIFFY THICK & QUICK 100% ACRYLIC 5 OZ (140 G) 84 YD (76 M) BALL

2 balls #207 Green Mountains or color of your choice

• Size P-15 (10 mm) crochet hook
or size to obtain gauge

GAUGE
9" (23 cm) from point to point + 3 rows = 4" (10 cm) over pattern stitch.
Be sure to check your gauge.

SCARF
Chain 142.
Row 1 Work 2 single crochet in the 2nd chain from the hook, single crochet in each of the next 5 chains, [insert hook in the next chain, yarn over and pull up a loop] 3 times, yarn over and draw through all 4 loops on the hook, single crochet in each of the next 5 chains, [work 3 single crochet in the next chain, single crochet in each of the next 5 chains, decrease over the next 3 chains, single crochet in each of the the next 5 chains] 9 times, work 2 single crochet in the last chain. Chain 4, turn.
Row 2 Treble crochet in the first single crochet, treble crochet in the next 5 single crochet, [yarn over twice, insert hook in the next single crochet, yarn over and pull up a loop, yarn over and draw through 2 loops, yarn over and draw through 2 loops again] 3 times, yarn over and draw through all 4 loops on hook—treble crochet decrease made, treble crochet in each of the next 5 single crochet, [work 3 treble crochet in the next single crochet, treble crochet in each of the next

5 single crochet, treble crochet decrease over the next 3 stitches, treble crochet in each of the next 5 single crochet] 9 times, work 2 treble crochet in the last single crochet. Chain 1, turn.

Row 3 Work 2 single crochet in the first treble crochet, single crochet in each of the next 5 treble crochet, [insert hook in the next treble crochet, yarn over and pull up a loop] 3 times, yarn over and draw through all 4 loops on the hook—decrease made, single crochet in each of the next 5 treble crochet, [work 3 single crochet in the next treble crochet, single crochet in each of the next 5 treble crochet, decrease over the next 3 stitches, single crochet in each of the next 5 treble crochet] 9 times, work 2 single crochet in the last treble crochet. Fasten off.

FINISHING
Weave in ends.

6.
LACE BASICS

Banish the thought of formal, white lace! Today's lace is colorful and decidedly unstuffy. Creating lace is the process of making decorative holes in knitted or crocheted fabric by increasing and decreasing regularly. In addition to creating traditional "lacy" patterns, lace techniques can be used to elongate the stitches of novelty yarns or lighten bulky fabrics.

It is advisable to place a marker between the pattern repeats to keep track of where you are on a row. Patterns are either written out row by row (using a series of abbreviations) or are expressed in chart form. Charts make life easier for the knitter or crocheter. Each box in a chart represents a stitch and different symbols are used to tell the knitter what to do. A key supplies explanations for each of the symbols in the chart and what to do when you are on a right or wrong side row. (For example, an empty box is the symbol for stockinette stitch: knit on the right side, purl on the wrong side.) Charts are read right to left on odd rows and left to right on even rows. To keep your place, put a ruler beneath the row you are working on.

KNITTING LACE

Lace patterns are created when a series of yarn overs and left- and/or right-slanting decreases are repeated across a row for a series of rows. The most commonly used method of increasing in lace knitting is called a yarn over (yo). Yarn overs are made by wrapping the yarn around (or *over*) the needle between stitches. This is how it's done:

Bring the yarn between the needles, wrapping the yarn counter-clockwise around the right needle and knit the next stitch (illustration 1-1). On the next row treat the yarn over as a normal stitch, knitting or purling it as the pattern dictates (illustration 1-2). A small hole or eyelet will form below the stitch.

In lace knitting, there are two methods of decreasing commonly used. The first technique is called knit 2 together (k2tog), which is done exactly how it is stated. This technique is worked as follows: Insert the right needle into the first

two stitches on the left needle, wrap the yarn around the needle the way you normally would, pulling the yarn through the two stitches (illustration 2-1). The two stitches will fall off the needle, leaving one new stitch on the right needle. This is also called a right-slanted decrease because the knit 2 together stitches slant to the right.

To create a left-slanted decrease, patterns often use a technique called slip, slip, knit (ssk). Work as follows: Insert the right needle tip into the first stitch on the left needle as if you were going to knit it and then slip it to the right needle without working it (illustration 3-1), slip the second stitch the same way. Insert the tip of the left needle into the front of the two slipped stitches (illustration 3-2), wrap the yarn around the right needle as you normally would and knit the two stitches off the needle.

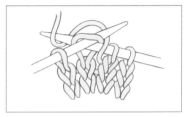

1-1. Make a yarn over by laying the yarn over the needle.

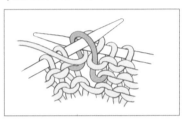

1-2. On the next row, work the strand as a stitch.

RIGHT-SLANTED DECREASE

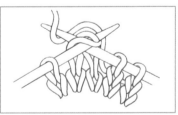

2-1. Knit 2 together decrease.

LEFT-SLANTED DECREASE

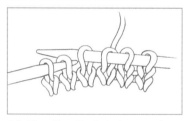

3-1. The slip, slip, knit decrease is made by slipping 2 stitches.

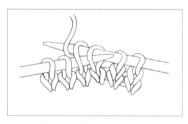

3-2. Knit the 2 slipped stitches in the front of the stitch.

CROCHETING LACE

Openwork or lace is made by leaving a space (hole) in the work and balancing increases and decreases (detailed instructions are on page 65). You can also produce an airy fabric by using an enormous hook and thin yarn.

Filet Crochet (sometimes called Irish Lace) is one of the easiest lace patterns to master. Boxes are created by chaining the same number of stitches as you have skipped in the previous row. The more chains you skip, the larger the hole.

RIBBON EFFECT

DESIGNED BY JENNIFER WERTKIN

KNIT/BEGINNER

This scarf gives you the look of lace in elegant, shiny ribbon. Garter stitch worked on big needles plus a simple technique to elongate the stitches provides maximum impact for minimum effort.

SIZE
3" x 73" (7.5 x 185 cm) (not including fringe)

MATERIALS

 LION BRAND YARN INCREDIBLE 100% POLYAMIDE 1¾ OZ (50 G) 110 YD (100 M) BALL

2 balls #205 Carnival or color of your choice

• Size 19 (15 mm) needles *or size to obtain gauge*

• Size J-10 (6 mm) crochet hook for fringe

GAUGE
17 stitches + 9 rows = 4" (10 cm) over pattern stitch.
Be sure to check your gauge.

PATTERN STITCH
Row 1 Knit.
Row 2 *Knit 1, yarn over; repeat from *, ending knit 1.
Row 3 *Knit 1 dropping the yarn over; repeat from * across the row, ending knit 1.
Row 4 Knit.
Repeat Rows 1–4 for pattern stitch.

SCARF
Cast on 13 stitches.
Knit the next row.
Begin pattern stitch and work even until the piece measures approximately 72" (183 cm) from beginning, ending with Row 4.
Knit the next row.
Bind off all stitches loosely as if to knit.

FINISHING
Weave in ends.
FRINGE
Follow directions for fringe on page 14.

SEASIDE DIAGONAL

DESIGNED BY CHARLOTTE QUIGGLE

KNIT/INTERMEDIATE

This scarf takes only two skeins, so you'll quickly be wearing this beauty. A garter stitch base makes it beautiful and reversible.

SIZE
6" x 60" (15 x 153 cm)

MATERIALS

 LION BRAND YARN LANDSCAPES
50% WOOL, 50% ACRYLIC 1¾ OZ
(50 G) 55 YD (50 M) BALL

2 balls #272 Pastel Meadow or color of your choice

• Size 10.5 (6.5 mm) knitting
  needles *or size to obtain gauge*

GAUGE
10 stitches + 20 rows = 4" (10 cm) over pattern.
Be sure to check your gauge.

NOTE
• Slip the first stitch of each row as if to purl with the yarn in front.

SCARF
Cast on 16 stitches. Knit 2 rows.
Row 1 (Right Side) Slip 1, knit 5, knit 2 together, yarn over, knit 4, knit 2 together, yarn over, knit 2.

Row 2 and All Wrong Side Rows Slip 1, knit to end.
Row 3 Slip 1, knit 4, knit 2 together, yarn over, knit 4, knit 2 together, yarn over, knit 3.
Row 5 Slip 1, knit 3, knit 2 together, yarn over, knit 4, knit 2 together, yarn over, knit 4.
Row 7 Slip 1, knit 2, knit 2 together, yarn over, knit 4, knit 2 together, yarn over, knit 5.
Row 9 Slip 1, knit 1, knit 2 together, yarn over, knit 4, knit 2 together, yarn over, knit 6.
Row 11 Slip 1, knit 2 together, yarn over, knit 4, knit 2 together, yarn over, knit 4, knit 2 together, yarn over, knit 1.
Row 12 Slip 1, knit to end.
Repeat Rows 1–12 until piece measures approximately 59½" (151 cm) from beginning, ending with a wrong side row.
Knit 2 rows. Bind off all stitches as if to knit. Weave in ends.

STITCH PATTERN

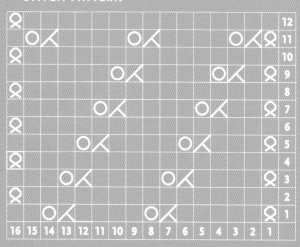

STITCH KEY

 Knit

♀ Slip stitch

⟋ Knit 2 together (K2TOG)

O Yarn over (YO)

KNIT/INTERMEDIATE

LILAC LACE

DESIGNED BY MARIANNE FORRESTAL

CROCHET/INTERMEDIATE

Filet crochet and an interesting picot edge make a pretty, versatile wrap with many wearing options.

SIZE
24" x 72" (61 x 183 cm)

MATERIALS

 LION BRAND YARN BABYSOFT 60% ACRYLIC, 40% NYLON 5 OZ (140 G) 459 YD (420 M) BALL

2 balls #143 Lavender or color of your choice

• Size I-9 (5.5 mm) crochet hook *or size to obtain gauge*

GAUGE

17 stitches + 7 rows = 4" (10 cm) over pattern stitch.
Be sure to check your gauge.

PATTERN STITCH

PICOT

In the same stitch work [3 double crochet, chain 3, slip stitch in the 3rd chain from the hook, 3 double crochet].

SHAWL

Chain 98.

Row 1 Double crochet in the 6th chain from the hook, *chain 1, skip the next chain, double crochet in the next chain; repeat from * 46 times. Chain 4 (counts as the first double crochet and the first chain-1 space of the next row), turn.

Row 2 Skip the first chain-1 space, *double crochet in the next double crochet, chain 1, skip the next chain-1 space; repeat from * across row, end with double crochet in the 4th chain of the starting chain-5. Chain 4, turn.

Row 3 Skip the first chain-1 space, *double crochet in the next double crochet, chain 1, skip the next chain-1 space; repeat from * across row, end with double crochet in the 3rd chain of the starting chain-4. Chain 4, turn.

Rows 4–127 Repeat Row 3. At the end of Row 127, chain 3. Do not fasten off.

FINISHING

Work 2 double crochet in the corner space. Working along the long edge of the shawl, work as follows: [single crochet in the next space, (skip the next space, picot in the next space, skip the next space, single crochet in the next space) 31 times, picot in the corner space.
Working along the short edge of the shawl, single crochet in the next space, (skip the next space, picot in the next space, skip the next space, single crochet in the next space) 11 times], picot in the corner space; repeat between [ ] once more, ending with (3 double crochet, chain 3, slip stitch in the third chain from the hook) all in the beginning corner space. Join the round with a slip stitch in the top of the starting chain-3. Fasten off. Weave in ends.

PINEAPPLE SCARF

DESIGNED BY DORIS CHAN

CROCHET/EXPERIENCED

This narrow scarf is light enough to be worn indoors while the bold lace motifs show off your crochet skills. With a pull-through slit to keep it in place, this scarf is the ideal dressy accessory.

SIZE

8" wide at widest point x 36" (20.5 x 91 cm)

MATERIALS

 LION BRAND YARN COLOR WAVES 83% ACRYLIC, 17% POLYESTER 3 OZ (85 G) 125 YD (113 M) SKEIN

1 skein #307 Caribbean or color of your choice

• Size K-10.5 (6.5 mm) crochet hook *or size to obtain gauge*

GAUGE

10.75 stitches + 8 rows = 4" (10 cm) over single crochet.
One pineapple motif = 8" wide by 7½" long (20.5 x 19 cm).
Be sure to check your gauge.

PATTERN STITCH

BASE CHAIN/SINGLE CROCHET

(**Note** This method creates a base chain and foundation row of single crochet at the same time; easy, sturdy, and elastic, especially useful for necklines and waistlines.)
Start with a slip knot, chain 2, insert the hook in the 2nd chain from the hook, draw up a loop, yarn over, draw through 1 loop, yarn over and draw through 2 loops—1 single crochet with its own chain at the bottom. Work the next stitch under the loops of that chain. Insert hook under 2 loops at the bottom of the previous stitch, draw up a loop, yarn over and draw through 1 loop, yarn over and draw through 2 loops. Repeat from chain 2 for length of foundation.

SHELL

Work (2 double crochet, chain 2, 2 double crochet) in same stitch or space.

JOIN YARN WITH A SINGLE CROCHET

Make a slip knot and place on the hook. Insert the hook into a foundation loop. Yarn over and draw up a loop. Yarn over and draw through 2 loops on hook.

SCARF

FOUNDATION ROW

Base chain/single crochet 8.

BEGIN FIRST PINEAPPLE MOTIF

Row 1 (Right Side) Chain 3 (counts as first double crochet), work (double crochet, chain 2, 2 double crochet) in the first single crochet, chain 2, double crochet in the next 6 double crochet, chain 2, Work shell in the last single crochet. Turn.
Row 2 Chain 2, work shell in the

first chain-2 space, chain 2, skip the next chain-2 space, double crochet in the next double crochet, [chain 1, double crochet in the next double crochet] 5 times, chain 2, skip the next chain-2 space, work shell in the last chain-2 space. Turn.

Row 3 Chain 2, work shell in the first chain-2 space, chain 2, skip the next chain-2 space, single crochet in the next chain-1 space, [chain 3, single crochet in the next chain-1 space] 4 times, chain 2, skip the next chain-2 space, work shell in the last chain-2 space. Turn.

Row 4 Chain 2, work shell in the first chain-2 space, chain 2, skip the next chain-2 space, single crochet in the next chain-3 space, [chain 3, single crochet in the next chain-3 space] 3 times, chain 2, skip the next chain-2 space, work shell in the last chain-2 space. Turn.

Row 5 Chain 2, work shell in the first chain-2 space, chain 2, skip the next chain-2 space, single crochet in the next chain-3 space, [chain 3, single crochet in the next chain-3 space] twice, chain 2, skip the next chain-2 space, work shell in the last chain-2 space. Turn.

Row 6 Chain 2, work shell in the first chain-2 space, chain 2, skip the next chain-2 space, single crochet in the next chain-3 space, chain 3, single crochet in the next chain-3 space, chain 2, skip the next chain-2 space, work shell in the last chain-2 space. Turn.

Row 7 Chain 2, work shell in the first chain-2 space, chain 2, skip the next chain-2 space, single crochet in the next chain-3 space, chain 2, skip the next chain-2 space, work shell in last chain-2 space. Turn.

Row 8 Chain 2, work 2 double crochet in the first chain-2 space, skip the next (chain-2 space, single crochet and chain-2 space), work 2 double crochet in the last chain-2 space, chain 2, slip stitch in the last double crochet. Fasten off.

NECKBAND
Position pineapple motif so the right side is facing and the bottom loops of the base chain are at the top.

SLIT OPENING
Next Row (Right Side) Join yarn with a single crochet in first loop, then single crochet in the next 3 loops—4 stitches. Chain 1, turn. Work even in single crochet for 2" (5 cm), ending with a wrong side row. Fasten off.

Next Row (Right Side) Join yarn with a single crochet in the next unworked loop of the foundation chain, then single crochet in the last 3 loops—4 stitches. Work even in single crochet for 2" (5 cm), ending with a wrong side row.

Joining Row (Right Side) Single crochet in the first 4 stitches, then with the same strand of yarn, single crochet in the next 4 stitches of the opposite side—8 stitches. Chain 1, turn. Continue to work in single crochet until the neckband measures 21" (53 cm) from beginning (28½" [72 cm] including the pineapple motif), ending with a wrong side row. Beginning with Row 1, work 2nd pineapple motif same as for first motif. Fasten off.

FINISHING
Weave in ends.

7.
REVERSIBLE SCARVES

One of the challenges of making scarves is that both sides are visible. The four scarves in this chapter look great no matter how you tie them. Rugged and Reversible uses a clever slip-stitch technique that makes each side look different. Denim Tweed uses a multicolored yarn as the main color and alternates striped solids to create a menswear-inspired look. Basketweaves are great stitches for scarves. Done in a thinner yarn, Basketweave Beauty would look great on a guy. On the Green uses a quick-to-crochet afghan technique.

BASKETWEAVE BEAUTY

DESIGNED BY TRACI BUNKERS

KNIT/EASY

Bold texture is achieved by a simple knit and purl pattern. The bulky yarn makes it extra cozy.

SIZE
9" x 71" (23 x 180 cm)

MATERIALS

 LION BRAND YARN WOOL-EASE THICK & QUICK 80% ACRYLIC, 20% WOOL 6 OZ (170 G) 108 YD (98 M) BALL

3 balls #187 Goldenrod or color of your choice

• Size 13 (9 mm) needles *or size to obtain gauge*

• Stitch marker

GAUGE
10 stitches + 14 rows = 4" (10 cm) over pattern.
Be sure to check your gauge.

SCARF
Cast on 24 stitches.

Row 1 Knit 1, [knit 4, purl 2, knit 1, purl 2] twice, knit 4, purl 1. Mark this row as the right side.

Row 2 Knit 1, [purl 4, knit 2, purl 1, knit 2] twice, purl 4, knit 1.

Rows 3–6 Repeat Rows 1–2 twice more.

Row 7 Repeat Row 2.

Row 8 Repeat Row 1.

Rows 9–10 Repeat Rows 7–8 once more.

Repeat Rows 1–10 for pattern stitch.

Work even in pattern stitch until the piece measures approximately 71" (180 cm) from beginning, ending with Row 6. Bind off all stitches as if to knit.

FINISHING
Weave in ends.

RUGGED AND REVERSIBLE

DESIGNED BY CHARLOTTE QUIGGLE

KNIT/INTERMEDIATE

The knit slip stitch lets you mix yarns in an unusual way: each yarn stands alone on one side of the scarf. Using a solid yarn with a variegated one emphasizes the contrast.

SIZE
6" x 60" (15 x 153 cm)

MATERIALS

LION BRAND YARN HOMESPUN 98% ACRYLIC, 2% POLYESTER 6 OZ (170 G) 185 YD (167 M) SKEIN

1 skein #302 Colonial (MC) or color of your choice

LION BRAND YARN LION BOUCLÉ 79% ACRYLIC, 20% MOHAIR, 1% NYLON 2½ OZ (70 G) 57 YD (52 M) BALL

1 ball #206 Hazelnut (CC) or color of your choice

• Size 10.5 (6.5 mm) circular needle *or size to obtain gauge*

GAUGE
15 stitches + 24 rows = 4" (10 cm) over pattern stitch.
Be sure to check your gauge.

SCARF
With MC, cast on 23 stitches. Work in pattern stitch and color pattern as follows:

Row 1 With MC, knit 1, *purl 1, knit 1; repeat from * to end. Turn.

Row 2 With CC, *slip 1 with yarn in front, knit 1; repeat from * to last stitch, ending slip 1 with yarn in front. Slide stitches to end of needle.

Row 3 With MC, *purl 1, slip 1 with yarn in back; repeat from * to last stitch, ending purl 1. Turn.

Row 4 Repeat Row 1. Slide.

Row 5 With CC, *slip 1 with yarn in back, purl 1; repeat from * to last stitch, ending slip 1 with yarn in back. Turn.

Row 6 With MC, *purl 1, slip 1 with yarn in back; repeat from * to last stitch, ending purl 1. Turn.

Repeat these 6 rows until piece measures approximately 60" (153 cm) from beginning, ending with Row 1 or 4. Bind off very loosely as follows: purl 2 together, *purl 2 together, bind off 1 stitch; repeat from * to last stitch, end purl 1, bind off 1 stitch. Fasten off.

FINISHING
Weave in ends.

ON THE GREEN

DESIGNED BY DORIS CHAN

CROCHET/EASY

This scarf shows how well differently textured yarns work together, combining a brushed acrylic yarn with two different bouclés. The unusual curved ends are a unique, appealing detail.

SIZE
6" x 80" (15 x 203 cm)

MATERIALS

 LION BRAND YARN JIFFY 100% ACRYLIC 2½ OZ (70 G) 115 YD (105 M) BALL

1 ball #111 Heather Blue (A) or color of your choice

 LION BRAND YARN LION BOUCLÉ 79% ACRYLIC, 20% MOHAIR, 1% NYLON 2½ OZ (70 G) 57 YD (52 M) BALL

1 ball #202 Lime Blue (B) or color of your choice

 LION BRAND YARN HOMESPUN 98% ACRYLIC, 2% POLYESTER 6 OZ (170 G) 185 YD (167 M) SKEIN

1 skein #369 Florida Keys Green (C) or color of your choice

• Size N-13 (9 mm) crochet hook
or size to obtain gauge

GAUGE
6 stitches = 4" (10 cm) over double crochet.
Be sure to check your gauge.

SCARF
With A, chain 119.

Foundation Row (Wrong Side)
Double crochet in the 7th chain from the hook and in each chain to within the last chain stitch, end row with chain 3, slip stitch in last chain—112 double crochet and 2 chain loops at each end (oval ends). Fasten off. Turn.

Round 1 Join B with a slip stitch in the chain-3 space, chain 3 (always counts as 1 double crochet), work 5 double crochet in the same chain-3 space, double crochet in each stitch of foundation row, then work 6 double crochet in the next chain-3 space. Turn work to the bottom loops of the foundation row, then double crochet in each loop across. Join round with a slip stitch in the third chain of the beginning chain-3. Fasten off. Turn.

Round 2 Join C with a slip stitch in the same stitch as joining, chain 3, double crochet in each stitch to the first oval end, work 2 double crochet in the next 6 stitches for oval end, double crochet in each stitch to the next oval end, work 2 double crochet in next 5 stitches of oval end, double crochet in the same stitch as beginning. Join round with a slip stitch in the third chain of the beginning chain-3. Fasten off. Turn.

Round 3 Join A with a slip stitch in the same stitch as joining, chain 3, [work 2 double crochet in next stitch, double crochet in the next stitch] 5 times, work 2 double

crochet in the last stitch of the first oval end, double crochet in each stitch to the next oval end, [double crochet in the next stitch, work 2 double crochet in the next stitch] 6 times, double crochet in each stitch to end. Join the round with a slip stitch in the third chain of the beginning chain-3. Fasten off.

FINISHING
Weave in ends.

DENIM TWEED

DESIGNED BY VLADIMIR TERIOKHAN

CROCHET/INTERMEDIATE

Using patterned yarn in a slip stitch design produces a tweedy fabric that he will love.

SIZE
5³/₄" x 48" (14.5 x 122 cm)

MATERIALS

 LION BRAND YARN MAGIC STRIPES 75% SUPERWASH WOOL, 25% NYLON 3¹/₂ OZ (100 G) 330 YD (302 M) BALL

1 ball #205 Brown/Blue Pattern (A) or color of your choice

 LION BRAND YARN WOOL-EASE 80% ACRYLIC, 20% WOOL 3 OZ (85 G) 197 YD (180 M) BALL

1 ball each #402 Wheat (B), #125 Camel (C), or colors of your choice

- Size G-6 (4 mm) crochet hook *or size to obtain gauge*

GAUGE
20 stitches + 19 rows = 4" (10 cm) over pattern stitch.
Be sure to check your gauge.

NOTES
- Use 2 strands of A held together throughout.

- Wind A into 4 separate balls and B and C into 2 separate balls each.

- Stripes are only one row per color. To prevent having to cut and join colors every row, work using two balls of each color. Remember to use 2 strands of A held together.

- When changing colors, draw the new color through 2 loops on the hook to complete the last single crochet.

- Carry colors not in use along the edge of the work.

PATTERN STITCH
MULTIPLE OF 2 STITCHES + 1

Row 1 (Right Side) Single crochet in the first stitch, *single crochet in the next chain-1 space, chain 1; repeat from *, ending single crochet in the next chain-1 space, single crochet in the last stitch. Chain 1, turn.

Row 2 Single crochet in the first stitch, *chain 1, single crochet in the next chain-1 space; repeat from *, ending chain 1, single crochet in last stitch. Chain 1, turn.

Repeat Rows 1 and 2 for pattern stitch.

SCARF

With 2 strands of A held together, chain 30.

Foundation Row 1 Single crochet in the second chain from the hook and in each chain across—29 stitches. Chain 1, turn.

Foundation Row 2 Single crochet in the first stitch, *chain 1, skip next stitch, single crochet in the next stitch; repeat from * to end. Join B, chain 1, turn. Continue in pattern stitch and stripe pattern as follows: *1 row B, 1 row A, 1 row C and 1 row A; repeat from * to end. Work even until piece measures 48" (122 cm) from beginning.

Last Row Single crochet in each stitch and chain-1 space across. Fasten off.

FINISHING

Weave in ends.

DENIM TWEED

8.

FABULOUS SCARVES

Put your stitching skills to the test with these half-dozen beauties. With so many creative patterns to choose from and a bevy of techniques to master, you'll be the first on your block to refute the notion that scarves are for beginners only. The patterns in this chapter will have your friends and family begging for bobbles when they see you sporting the Swiss Miss Scarf and pleading for a touch of romance as only Vintage Vines can deliver. Those who have wanted to experiment with mitered construction will have two opportunities, in knit and crochet, with Jellybean Miters and Nefertiti Shawl, respectively. From the intarsia skills called upon in Gentleman Caller to the new lace-making heights featured in Gilt Complex, the patterns in this chapter will keep you stitching to your heart's content.

GENTLEMAN CALLER

DESIGNED BY WENDY PRESTON

KNIT/EASY

This is a great first intarsia project. Less adventurous knitters can simply knit two 9-stitch strips and sew them together afterward.

SIZE
6" x 60" (15 x 153 cm)

MATERIALS

 LION BRAND YARN KOOL WOOL 50% MERINO WOOL, 50% ACRYLIC 1¼ OZ (50 G) 60 YD (54 M) BALL

2 balls #110 Navy (MC) or color of your choice

 LION BRAND YARN COLOR WAVES 83% ACRYLIC, 17% POLYESTER 3 OZ (85 G) 125 YD (113 M) SKEIN

1 skein #350 Night Sky (CC) or color of your choice

- Size 10.5 (6.5 mm) knitting needles *or size to obtain gauge*

- Large-eyed, blunt needle

GAUGE
14 stitches = 4" (10 cm) over garter stitch (knit every row).
Be sure to check your gauge.

NOTES
- When changing colors, pick up the new color from under the dropped color to prevent holes.

SCARF
With MC, cast on 18 stitches.

BEGIN COLOR PATTERN

Next Row (Right Side) With MC, knit 9, with CC, knit 9. Maintaining the color pattern as established, work even in garter stitch until the piece measures 3" (8 cm) from the beginning, ending with a wrong side row.

Next Row (Right Side) With MC, knit 18.

Next Row With MC, knit 9, with CC, knit 9. Maintaining the color pattern as established, work even for 3" (8 cm), ending with a wrong side row.

Next Row (Right Side) With CC, knit 18.

Next Row With CC, knit 9, with MC, knit 9. Maintaining the color pattern as established, work even for 3" (8 cm), ending with a wrong side row.

Continue to alternate color blocks every 3" (8 cm) as established until the piece measures 60" (153 cm) from the beginning.

Bind off all stitches as if to knit with MC. Weave in ends.

FINISHING
Using MC, embroider a blanket stitch around the entire edge. See instructions on page 16.

GILT COMPLEX

DESIGNED BY CHARLOTTE QUIGGLE

KNIT/INTERMEDIATE

Leave your necklaces at home and don this dazzling scarf instead. Cascading lace motifs trim a knitted rib pattern for an elegant effect.

SIZE

7" at the widest point x 36" (18 x 91 cm)

MATERIALS

LION BRAND YARN GLITTERSPUN 60% ACRYLIC, 13% POLYESTER, 27% CUPRO 1¾ OZ (50 G) 115 YD (105 M) BALL

2 balls #153 Onyx (A), 1 ball #150 Silver (B), 1 ball #170 Gold (C), 1 ball #135 Bronze (D), or colors of your choice

- Size 8 (5 mm) needles—2 pair *or size to obtain gauge*

GAUGE

23 stitches + 26 rows = 4" (10 cm) over pattern stitch and border. *Be sure to check your gauge.*

NOTE

- Cravat is made in two pieces (called ends).

- Each end is made beginning at the bottom edge of the first tier.

- Ends are grafted together. (See Glossary, page 108.)

STITCH EXPLANATIONS

PATTERN STITCH AND BORDER (MULTIPLE OF 4 STITCHES + 3)

Row 1 (Right Side) Knit.

Row 2 Knit 2, *purl 3, knit 1; rep from *, ending purl 3, knit 2. Repeat Rows 1 and 2 for pattern stitch and border.

FIRST END

FIRST TIER

With B, cast on 57 stitches.

Row 1 (Right Side) Knit 2, *knit 1, slip this stitch back to the left needle, working one at a time, lift the next 8 stitches on the left needle up and over this stitch and off the needle, yarn over twice (see yarn over instructions, page 76), then knit the first stitch again, knit 2; repeat from * to end—27 stitches on the needle.

Row 2 Knit 1, *knit 2 together, drop one yarn over off the needle, work (purl 1, knit 1, purl 1, knit 1, purl 1) in the remaining yarn over, knit 1; repeat from *, ending knit 1—37 stitches on the needle.

Row 3 Knit 2, *purl 5, knit 2; repeat from * to end.

Rows 4, 6, and 8 Knit 2, purl to the last 2 stitches, knit 2.

Rows 5, 7, and 9 Knit.

Row 10 Repeat Row 4. Cut yarn leaving a long tail. Leave stitches on needle and set aside. Use a spare needle for the next tier.

SECOND TIER

Using C, work as for the first tier until Row 4 is completed.

JOINING TIERS

Row 5 (Right Side) With the right side facing, hold the needle with the first tier, parallel to and behind the needle with the second tier.

Using C, join tiers together as follows: *knit 1 stitch from front needle together with 1 stitch from back needle; repeat from * to end. Beginning with Row 6, continue to work same as for the first tier until Row 10 is completed. Cut yarn leaving a long tail. Set work aside.

THIRD TIER
Using D, work same as for the second tier.

FOURTH TIER
Using A, work same as for the second tier until Row 5 is completed.

Next Row (Wrong Side) Knit 2, *purl 5, knit 2; repeat from * to end.

Next Row Knit. Continue to work in the pattern stitch as established for 9 more rows, ending with a wrong side row.

Decrease Row (Right Side) Knit 2, *slip slip knit, knit 1, knit 2 together twice; repeat from *, ending slip slip knit, knit 1, knit 2 together, knit 2—23 stitches. Beginning with Row 2, work in the pattern stitch and border for 5 rows, ending with a wrong side row. Leave stitches on the needle; cut yarn leaving a 20" (51 cm) tail.

SECOND END
Work as for the first end until the decrease row of fourth tier is completed—23 stitches. Beginning with Row 2, work in the pattern stitch and border for 18 rows, ending with a right side row.

SLIT OPENING
Row 1 (Wrong Side) Knit 2, purl 3, knit 1, purl 3, knit 5, purl 3, knit 1, purl 3, knit 2.

Row 2 Knit.

Row 3 Repeat Row 1.

Row 4 (Right Side) Knit 11, join another strand of A and bind off the center stitch, knit to the end of the row.

Row 5 With the first strand of yarn, knit 2, purl 3, knit 1, purl 3, knit 2, with the second strand of yarn, knit 2, purl 3, knit 1, purl 3, knit 2.

Row 6 Knit across each side.

Repeat Rows 5 and 6 five times more, then Row 6 once.

Row 18 (Right Side) Knit 11, cast on 1 stitch, with the same strand of yarn, knit 11. Drop the second strand of yarn.

Row 19 Knit 2, purl 3, knit 1, purl 3, knit 5, purl 3, knit 1, purl 3, knit 2.

Row 20 Knit.

Row 21 Repeat Rows 1–19. Beginning with Row 1, work in the pattern stitch and border until the piece measures 32" (81 cm) from the beginning, ending with a wrong side row. Slip stitches to the spare needle; cut yarn.

FINISHING
Graft ends together following instructions on page 108. Weave in ends.

JELLYBEAN MITERS

DESIGNED BY TRACI BUNKERS

KNIT/INTERMEDIATE

Two strands of patterned yarn combine to create a unique-to-you color pattern when worked up in this appealing mitered scarf. The motifs are joined as you knit, so there's practically no finishing.

SIZE

5" x 65" (12.5 x 165 cm)

MATERIALS

LION BRAND YARN MAGIC STRIPES 75% SUPERWASH WOOL, 25% NYLON 3½ OZ (100 G) 330 YD (300 M) BALL

3 balls #200 Jelly Bean Stripe or color of your choice

- Size 8 (5 mm) knitting needles *or size to obtain gauge*

- Size H-8 (5 mm) crochet hook

GAUGE

18 stitches + 36 rows = 4" (10 cm) over garter stitch (knit every row) using 2 strands held together. *Be sure to check your gauge.*

NOTES

- Work with 2 strands of yarn held together throughout.

- Pick up all stitches along cast-on edges of indicated motifs.

- To "slip 2 stitches as if to knit" means you should transfer stitches knitwise from left to right, without actually knitting them.

- The combination of slipping stitches and passing the slipped stitches over the knit-1 stitches creates the mitered corners.

- Referring to the diagram on the next page, work/join motifs in the designated order to evenly distribute colors.

- All yarn ends will be hidden when you work the crocheted edging.

SCARF

MOTIF 1

With 2 strands of yarn held together, cast on 42 stitches.

Row 1 and All Wrong Side Rows Knit.

Row 2 (Right Side) Knit 9, [slip 2 stitches as if to knit, knit 1, pass slipped stitches over—S2KP2], knit 18, slip 2 stitches as if to knit, knit 1, pass slipped stitches over, knit 9—38 stitches.

Row 4 Knit 8, S2KP2, knit 16, S2KP2, knit 8—34 stitches.

Row 6 [Knit to 1 stitch before the decrease, S2KP2] twice, knit to end. Continue working the decreases as established every right side row until 6 stitches remain.

Next Right Side Row S2KP2 twice, pass the first stitch over the second stitch. Fasten off.

MOTIF 2

Cast on 10 stitches, then with the right side facing and working along the long cast-on edge of Motif 1, pick up and knit 1 stitch in a corner, 20 stitches along the edge and 1 stitch in the other corner, then cast on 10 stitches—42 stitches. Beginning with Row 1, work as for Motif 1.

MOTIF 3

With the right side facing, pick up and knit 10 stitches along the top edge of Motif 2, 1 stitch in Motif 2 corner, then cast on 31 stitches—42 stitches. Beginning with Row 1, work as for Motif 1.

MOTIF 4

Cast on 10 stitches, then with right side facing, pick up and knit 1 stitch in the top corner of Motif 3, 20 stitches along the cast-on edge to the other corner, 1 stitch in a corner and 10 stitches along the top edge of Motif 1—42 stitches. Beginning with Row 1, work as for Motif 1.

MOTIF 5

Cast on 31 stitches, then with the right side facing and working along the top of Motif 4, pick up and knit 1 stitch in a corner and 10 stitches along the top edge—42 stitches. Beginning with Row 1, work as for Motif 1.

MOTIF 6

With the right side facing, pick up and knit 10 stitches along the top edge of Motif 3, 1 stitch in Motif 5 corner, 20 stitches along the cast-on edge to the other corner, 1 stitch in the corner, then cast on 10 stitches—42 stitches. Beginning with Row 1, work as for Motif 1. Repeat Motifs 3–6 until there are 24 motifs total.

END TRIANGLE

With the right side facing, pick up and knit 21 stitches evenly spaced along one short end of the scarf (10 per motif and 1 in center). Knit next row.

Decrease Row (Right Side) Slip slip knit, knit to last 2 stitches, knit 2 together.

Next Row Knit. Repeat last 2 rows 8 times more—3 stitches.

Last Row (Right Side) S2KP2. Fasten off last stitch. Repeat for opposite end.

FINISHING

From the Right Side with a crochet hook and 2 strands of yarn, join yarns with a slip stitch in the point of an end triangle. Chain 1, single crochet between every garter ridge (working over the yarn ends to hide), to the opposite triangle point. Work 3 single crochet in this triangle point, then work a single crochet between every garter ridge to the beginning triangle point, work 2 more single crochet in this

triangle point. Join round with a slip stitch in the beginning chain-1. Fasten off. Weave in ends.

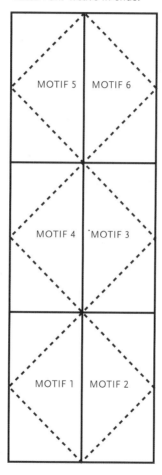

——— CAST ON EDGE
——— ROW EDGE
- - - - - S2KP2

SWISS MISS SCARF

DESIGNED BY VLADIMIR TERIOKHAN

CROCHET/EASY

Crocheted bobbles are a charming touch on the perfect winter scarf. The pull-through slit means you'll never have to fuss with it, whether you're riding a toboggan or sitting pretty in an outdoor cafe.

SIZE
7" x 53" (18 x 135 cm)

MATERIALS

LION BRAND YARN KOOL WOOL 50% MERINO WOOL, 50% ACRYLIC 1¾ OZ (50 G) 60 YD (54 M) BALL

5 balls #098 Ivory or color of your choice

• Size K-10.5 (6.5 mm) crochet hook *or size to obtain gauge*

GAUGE
11 double crochet + 6 rows = 4" (10 cm). *Be sure to check your gauge.*

NOTES
• Bobbles are worked on the wrong side. Push the bobble through to the right side after completion.

• Beginning chain-1 for single crochet rows does not count as a single crochet.

STITCH EXPLANATION
BOBBLE

Work all in the same stitch: [Yarn over, insert hook in the stitch and draw up a loop, yarn over and draw through 2 loops] 4 times, yarn over, draw through all loops on hook—1 bobble made.

SCARF

Row 1 (Wrong Side) Chain 23, double crochet in the fourth chain from the hook and in each chain across—21 double crochet. Turn.

Row 2 Chain 3 (counts as 1 double crochet), double crochet in each double crochet across, double crochet in the top of the beginning chain-3. Turn.

Row 3 Chain 3, *chain 1, skip 1 stitch, bobble in the next stitch, chain 1, skip 1 stitch, double crochet in the next stitch; repeat from * across—5 bobbles. Turn.

Row 4 Chain 1, single crochet in the first stitch and in each stitch across. Turn.

Row 5 Chain 3, bobble in the next single crochet, *double crochet in the next single crochet, chain 1, skip 1 single crochet, bobble in the next single crochet, chain 1, skip 1 single crochet; repeat from * to the last 3 stitches, double crochet in the next single crochet, bobble in the next single crochet, double crochet in the last stitch—6 bobbles. Turn.

Rows 6–8 Work 1 row single crochet, 1 row double crochet, 1 row single crochet.

Row 9 Chain 3, double crochet in each of next 3 single crochet, chain 1, skip 1 single crochet, bobble in the next single crochet, chain 1, skip 1 single crochet, double crochet in each of the next 7 single crochet, chain 1, skip 1 single crochet, bobble in the next single crochet, chain 1, skip 1 single crochet, double crochet in each of the next 4 single crochet—2 bobbles. Turn.

Row 10 Work 1 row single crochet.

Row 11 Chain 3, [double crochet in the next single crochet, chain 1, skip 1 single crochet, bobble in the next single crochet, chain 1, skip 1 single crochet] twice, double crochet in each of the next 3 single crochet, [chain 1, skip 1 single crochet, bobble in the next single crochet, chain 1, skip 1 single crochet, double crochet in the next single crochet] twice, double crochet in last single crochet—4 bobbles. Turn.

Row 12 Work 1 row single crochet.

Row 13 Repeat Row 9.

Rows 14–16 Repeat Rows 6–8.

Row 17 Chain 3, double crochet in the next stitch, *chain 1, skip 1 stitch, bobble in the next stitch, chain 1, skip 1 stitch, double crochet in each of the next 2 stitches; repeat from * to the last 4 stitches; chain 1, skip 1 stitch, bobble in the next stitch, double crochet in each of the next 2 stitches—4 bobbles. Turn.

Rows 18–23 Work 6 rows double crochet.

BEGIN SLIT

RIGHT HALF

Row 24 Chain 3, double crochet in each of the next 10 stitches, turn work leaving the remaining stitches unworked.

Row 25 Chain 3, double crochet in each of the next 10 stitches. Turn.

Rows 26–28 Repeat Row 25 three times more. Remove the hook and cut the yarn leaving a tail, but do not fasten off—leave last loop open.

LEFT HALF

Row 24 With the right side facing and beginning on the first row of the slit, join the yarn in the next stitch. Chain 3, double crochet in each of the next 9 stitches. Turn.

Row 25 Chain 3, double crochet in each of the next 9 stitches. Turn.

Rows 26–28 Repeat Row 25 three times more. Remove the hook and insert it in the loop from the right half. Join with a slip stitch to the top of the beginning chain-3 on the left half of the slit to close. Fasten off. Insert the hook back in the loop at the end of the row. Turn. Work 33 rows of double crochet across all 21 stitches. Turn.

Repeat Rows 24–28 for a second slit, then work 6 rows of double crochet across all 21 stitches. Work Rows 17–3 in reverse order, then work 2 rows of double crochet. Fasten off.

FINISHING

Weave in ends.

VINTAGE VINES

DESIGNED BY LIDIA KARABINECH

CROCHET/INTERMEDIATE

A ribbed scarf embellished with crocheted flowers and embroidery radiates retro flair.

SIZE
7½" x 74" (19 x 188 cm) (not including fringe)

MATERIALS
 LION BRAND YARN WOOL-EASE 80% ACRYLIC, 20% WOOL 3 OZ (85 G) 197 YD (180 M) BALL

4 balls #152 Oxford Grey (A),
1 ball #139 Dark Rose Heather (B),
1 ball #140 Rose Heather (C),
1 ball #130 Green Heather (D), or colors of your choice

• Size J-10 (6 mm) crochet hook or size to obtain gauge

GAUGE
14 stitches + 8 rows = 4" (10 cm) over double crochet.
Be sure to check your gauge.

NOTE
• See instructions for back and front posts on page 108.

STITCH EXPLANATION
RIB PATTERN (MULTIPLE OF 2 STITCHES + 1)
Row 1 *Front post double crochet, back post double crochet; repeat from *, ending with a double crochet in the chain-3 space of the turning chain. Chain 3, turn. Repeat Row 1 for Rib Pattern.

SCARF
With MC, chain 27.
Row 1 Double crochet in the fourth chain from the hook and in each chain across—25 stitches. Chain 3, turn.
Row 2 Double crochet in each stitch across. Chain 3, turn. Repeat Row 2 until 13 rows have been completed from the beginning. Chain 3, turn.
Change to Rib Pattern and work even until piece measures 67" (170 cm) from the beginning. Chain 3, turn.

Work 13 rows double crochet. Fasten off. Weave in ends.

FLOWERS
Following the directions for crocheted flowers on page 17, make three with A and three with B. With the right side facing, sew 2 A flowers and 1 B flower to the double crochet section at the bottom of the scarf, and 1 A flower and 2 B flowers to the double crochet section at the top of scarf, as shown. With 2 strands of C, embroider chain-stitch stems as shown in photo or as desired.

FINISHING
Follow directions for fringe on page 14, making fringe 20" (51 cm) long.

NEFERTITI SHAWL

DESIGNED BY VLADIMIR TERIOKHAN

CROCHET/INTERMEDIATE

This mitered crochet showstopper is fit for a queen.

SIZE

12" x 56" (30.5 x 142 cm), excluding tassels

MATERIALS

 LION BRAND YARN LION CHENILLE 100% ACRYLIC 3 OZ (85 G) 174 YD (157 M) BALL

2 balls Black #153 (A), 1 ball Mocha #125 (B), or colors of your choice

 LION BRAND YARN GLITTERSPUN 60% ACRYLIC, 13% POLYESTER, 27% CUPRO 1¾ OZ (50 G) 115 YD (105 M) BALL

2 balls Onyx #153 (C), 2 balls Gold #170 (D), or colors of your choice

- Size I–9 (5.5mm) crochet hook *or size to obtain gauge*

- Large-eyed, blunt needle

GAUGE

1 square = 3" x 3" (7.5 x 7.5 cm). *Be sure to check your gauge.*

NOTE

- Carry unused color up the side edge of the square.

SQUARES—MAKE 32 USING A/C AND 27 USING B/D

Row 1 With Lion Chenille, chain 2, 3 single crochet in the first chain— 3 single crochet. Turn.

Row 2 Chain 1, single crochet in the first stitch, 3 single crochet in the next stitch (corner), single crochet in the last stitch, drop Lion Chenille—5 single crochet. Turn.

Row 3 With Glitterspun, chain 1, single crochet in the first 2 stitches, 3 single crochet in the corner stitch, single crochet in the next 2 stitches—7 stitches. Turn.

Row 4 Chain 1, single crochet in the first 3 stitches, 3 single crochet in the corner stitch, single crochet in the next 3 stitches, drop Glitterspun—9 stitches. Turn.

Row 5 With Lion Chenille, chain 1, single crochet in the first 4 stitches, 3 single crochet in the corner stitch, single crochet in the next 4 stitches—11 stitches. Turn.

Row 6 Chain 1, single crochet in the first 5 stitches, 3 single crochet in the corner stitch, single crochet in the next 5 stitches, drop Lion Chenille—13 stitches. Turn. Continue working in this way, increasing 2 stitches per row and alternating two rows of each yarn until 12 rows have been worked and there are 25 stitches total. Fasten off.

SCARF

With Glitterspun, sew squares together following the diagram, placing direction of each square as desired.

FINISHING

EDGING

Work 1 row of single crochet in Lion Chenille using the same color as the square on all edges that are

row edges. Edges that are part of
the last row of squares do not
need edging.

FRINGE—MAKE 14 BLACK AND
10 MOCHA
Cut 8 strands 11" (28 cm) long of
Lion Chenille for each fringe. Fold
fringe in half to form a loop. Insert
hook in corner edge of square of contrasting color and pull loop through.
Bring ends through loop and tighten.
(See page 14 for fringing.) Repeat on
all corner edges.

▨ BLACK/ONYX SQUARE
▨ MOCHA/GOLD SQUARE

NEFERTITI SHAWL

GLOSSARY

BACK POST DOUBLE CROCHET (BPDC): Yarn over, insert hook from back to front then to back, going around the double crochet post, draw up a loop (yarn over and draw through 2 loops on hook) twice. Skip stitch in front of the BPDC.

CC: Contrast color in a two-color scarf.

CHAIN: In crocheting, this is a loop made simply by drawing the yarn through an existing stitch or loop. It also refers to a series of loops; "chain 3" means to make three chain stitches in a row.

CN: Cable needle.

DOUBLE CROCHET (DC): This is a basic crochet stitch that is taller than a half double and shorter than a triple crochet stitch.

FRONT POST DOUBLE CROCHET (FPDC): Yarn over, insert hook from front to back then to front, going around the double crochet post, draw up a loop, (yarn over and draw through 2 loops on hook) twice. Skip stitch behind the FPDC.

GARTER STITCH: Knit every row.

GAUGE: Sometimes called tension, gauge is the number of stitches and rows measured over a number of inches (or centimeters).

GRAFTING: A technique for joining two rows of "live" stitches without a seam. To graft, hold the two needles with the live stitches on them parallel with wrong sides of fabric together. Thread a blunt tapestry needle with one of the yarn ends and work as follows: Insert tapestry needle as if to purl into the first stitch on the front piece. Insert needle as if to knit into the first stitch on the back piece. Then follow steps 1–4 as outlined below. (1) Insert needle as if to knit through the first stitch on front knitting needle and let the stitch drop from the needle. (2) Insert tapestry needle into 2nd stitch on the front needle as if to purl and pull the yarn through, leaving stitch on the knitting needle. (3) Insert tapestry needle into the first stitch on the back needle as if to purl and let it drop from the knitting needle, then (4) insert tapestry needle as if to knit through 2nd stitch on back needle and pull the yarn through, leaving the stitch on the knitting needle. Repeat 1–4 until all stitches are gone. When finished, adjust the tension as necessary. Weave in ends.

HALF DOUBLE CROCHET: A crochet stitch that is taller than a single crochet and shorter than double crochet.

KNIT 2 TOGETHER (K2TOG): A decrease made by inserting the needle into the first two stitches on the left needle, wrapping the yarn around as you normally would, and then pulling the yarn through both stitches. See illustrations on page 76.

LEFT-SLANTED DECREASE: See knit 2 together.

MAKE 1: An increase worked by lifting the horizontal thread lying between the needles and placing it on the left needle. Work this new stitch through the back loop.

MC: Main color in a two-color scarf.

RIGHT-SLANTED DECREASE: See slip, slip, knit.

SINGLE CROCHET (SC): A basic crochet stitch that is taller than a slip stitch and shorter than a half double crochet.

SLIDE: Push stitches back to opposite end of needle and, keeping the same side of the fabric facing, work the next row.

SLIP, SLIP, KNIT (SSK): Slip next two stitches as if to knit, one at a time, to the right needle; insert left needle into the fronts of these two stitches and knit them together. See illustrations on page 76.

S2KP2: Slip 2 sts as if to knit, knit 1, pass 2 slipped stitches over.

STOCKINETTE STITCH: Knit one row, purl one row.

TRIPLE (TREBLE) CROCHET: This is the tallest of all the basic crochet stitches.

TURN: Turn needle around and, with opposite side of fabric facing, work the next row.

WHIPSTITCH: A decorative seaming technique. Using either matching or contrasting yarn, bring needle through the fabric of one piece to be joined from wrong side to right side. Insert needle back through the fabric of the other piece and pull yarn carefully, avoiding pulling stitches too tightly. Repeat to end of fabric.

YARN OVER (YO): An increase created by wrapping the yarn counterclockwise around the right-hand needle and knitting the next stitch.

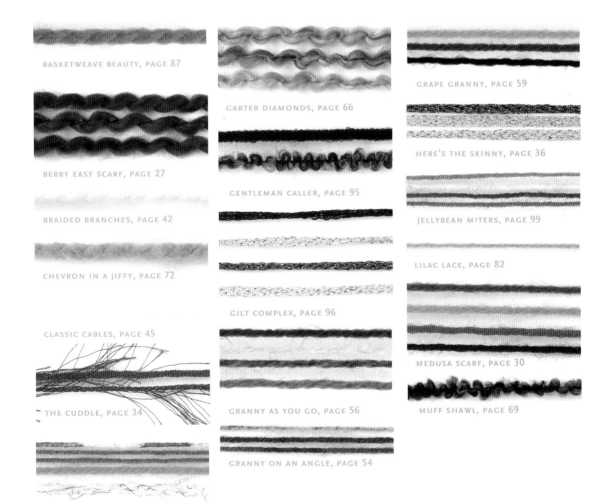

BASKETWEAVE BEAUTY, PAGE 87

BERRY EASY SCARF, PAGE 27

BRAIDED BRANCHES, PAGE 42

CHEVRON IN A JIFFY, PAGE 72

CLASSIC CABLES, PAGE 45

THE CUDDLE, PAGE 34

DENIM TWEED, PAGE 92

GARTER DIAMONDS, PAGE 66

GENTLEMAN CALLER, PAGE 95

GILT COMPLEX, PAGE 96

GRANNY AS YOU GO, PAGE 56

GRANNY ON AN ANGLE, PAGE 54

GRAPE GRANNY, PAGE 59

HERE'S THE SKINNY, PAGE 36

JELLYBEAN MITERS, PAGE 99

LILAC LACE, PAGE 82

MEDUSA SCARF, PAGE 30

MUFF SHAWL, PAGE 69

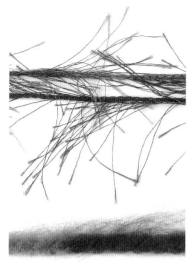

NEFERTITI SHAWL, 106

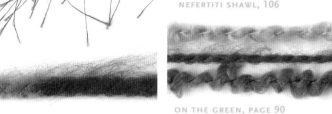

ON THE GREEN, PAGE 90

RIBBON EFFECT, PAGE 79

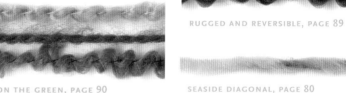

RUGGED AND REVERSIBLE, PAGE 89

SEASIDE DIAGONAL, PAGE 80

OUTRAGEOUS CABLED COLLAR, PAGE 48

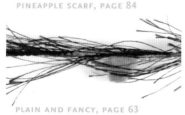

PINEAPPLE SCARF, PAGE 84

SWISS MISS SCARF, PAGE 102

MY SCARF, MY WAY!
CROCHET SCARF, PAGE 23

TIE BEAUX, PAGE 24

MY SCARF MY WAY!
KNIT SCARF, PAGE 20

PLAIN AND FANCY, PAGE 63

VINTAGE VINES, PAGE 105

POCKET POSSIBILITIES, PAGE 33

WESTERN WEAVE, PAGE 39

111

INDEX

Basketweave Beauty, 87
Berry Easy Scarf, 26–27
Blanket stitch, 16
Braided Branches, 42–43
Bunkers, Traci, 30–31, 87, 98–101

Cables, 40–49
Chain stitch, 16
Chan, Doris, 84–85, 91–92
Charts
    cable, 41
    reading, 19
Chevron in a Jiffy, 72–73
Children, scarves for, 13
Classic Cables, 45–47
Colors, changing, 28
Craft Yarn Council of America, 9
Crochet
    beginner patterns for, 9, 22–23,
        26–27, 36–37
    easy patterns for, 9, 36–39, 54–57,
        72–73, 90–91, 103–4
    experienced patterns for, 9, 84–85
    flowers, 17
    increasing and decreasing in, 62,
        65
    intermediate patterns for, 9, 58–61,
        82–83, 92–93, 104–105, 106–107
    lace, 77
The Cuddle, 34–35

Denim Tweed, 86, 92–93

Embellishments, 14
Embroidery, 16

Fabulous scarves, 94–107
Finishing, 13
Flowers, 17
Forrestal, Marianne, 26–27, 36–37,
    54–57, 72–73, 82–83

Fringe, 14
Fun finishes, 14–17

Garter Diamonds, 66–67
Gauges, 10–12
Gentleman Caller, 95
Gilt Complex, 94, 96–97
Granny on an Angle, 54–55
Granny As You Go, 56–57
Granny squares, 50–61
Grape Granny, 58–61

Here's the Skinny, 36–37
Hooks, 10–11, 12

Jellybean Miters, 94, 98–101

Karabinech, Lidia, 58–61, 104–105
Klose, Stephanie, 66–67
Knitting
    beginner patterns for, 9, 20–21,
        24–25, 78–79
    easy patterns for, 9, 30–31, 42–43,
        48–49, 63, 66–67, 87, 95
    flowers, 17
    increasing and decreasing in, 62,
        64
    intermediate patterns for, 9, 44–47,
        68–71, 80–81, 88–89, 96–101
    lace, 76

Lace basics, 74–85
Lilac Lace, 82–83

Medusa Scarf, 30–31
Mighty Mini, 29
Muff Shawl, 68–71
My Scarf, My Way!, 18, 20–23

Needles, 9, 10–11
Nefertiti Shawl, 94, 106–107

On the Green, 86, 90–91
Outrageous Cabled Collar, 48–49

Peterson, Gabrielle, 34–35
Picot borders, 17

Pineapple Scarf, 84–85
Plain and Fancy, 63
Pocket Possibilities, 32–33
Pom-poms, 15
Preston, Wendy, 24–25, 32–33, 95

Quiggle, Charlotte, 80–81, 88–89, 96–97

Reversible scarves, 86–93
Ribbon Effect, 78–79
Rings, joining, 53
Rosen, Rebecca, 63
Rugged and Reversible, 86, 88–89

Seam, slip stitch, 53
Seaside Diagonal, 80–81
Sizing, 13
Swiss Miss, 94, 102–103

Tassels, 15
Teriokhan, Vladimir, 38–39, 48–49,
    68–71, 92–93, 102–103, 106–107
Tie Beaux, 22–23
Tools, 10–11, 12

Vintage Vines, 94, 105

Weaving, 16
Wertkin, Jennifer, 78–79
Western Weave, 26, 38–39

Yarns, knowing, 10

Zimmerman, Kathy, 42–47